How to MEMORIZE
NAMES, NUMBERS, SPEECHES, PLAYING CARDS *and EVERYTHING ELSE*

Visit
www.BrainAthlete.com
and enter your email address
to get our free training on remembering names

How to Memorize

NAMES, NUMBERS, SPEECHES, PLAYING CARDS and EVERYTHING ELSE
By Ron White

U..S.A. Memory Champion & Memory Record Holder

www.BrainAthlete.com

Published by

ron@brainathlete.com   ❍   (972) 801-5330

White, Ron, HOW TO MEMORIZE NAMES, NUMBERS, SPEECHES, PLAYING CARDS and EVERYTHING ELSE

International Standard Book Number: **ISBN 978-0-9747212-4-8**

Printed in the United States of America.

First Printing, March 2010

Book Cover Design by Joni McPherson, McPherson Graphics
Book Interior Design by Kevin Haislip/HaislipCreative

Table of Contents

Day 1 — Intro to Memory Training   page 5

Day 2 — Basic Association   page 10

Day 3— Chain of Visualization   page 20

Day 4—A 2000 Year Old Memory Method   page 25

Day 5—Skeleton Files   page 34

Day 6— Pencil List Practice   page 40

Day 7— Counting in Japanese   page 43

Day 8— Memorizing Math Formulas   page 48

Day 9— Creating Your House Files   page 52

Day 10— Poems and Quotes   page 55

Day 11— Memorizing Sales Presentations   page 60

Day 12—Uses For Files   page 63

Day 13—Giving Speeches Without Notes   page 66

Day 14— Foreign Languages   page 70

Day 15— Intro to Number Memory   page 74

Day 16— How to memorize Numbers   page 81

Day 17— Pictures for Numbers to 1000   page 84

Day 18— Memorizing the Presidents   page 93

Day 19— Names and Faces   page 99

Day 20— Names and Faces   page 103

Day 21—Names and Faces   page 110

Day 22— Fun Memory Demonstrations   page 114

Day 23— Memorizing a Deck of Cards   page 117

Day 24— Memorizing Scripture   page 120

Day 25—Working on Speed Memory   page 125

Day 26— Things To Do, Directions, Names   page 127

Day 27— Memorizing Sub-Points   page 130

Day 28—Alphabet Files   Page 133

Day 29—Keep Your Motivation Up!   Page 135

Day 30—Review and a New Beginning   page 139

day 1

Intro to Memory Training

Hello, and welcome to our How to Memorize EVERYTHING program! Psychologists tell us that if we do anything for 21 or more days, it will become a habit. This program is carefully designed to help you make instant recall memory a habit. What you have in your hands is what I believe to be the most comprehensive program of its nature. Enjoy it.

This program is divided into 30 sections to be completed in thirty days , however you may progress at your own pace. It should take you about ten minutes a day. If you get excited and want to do more than one lesson in a day there is certainly no harm in that!

We will start out very basic. Don't get bored during the simple stuff. Believe it or not, the simple basics are going to be the foundation for the advanced techniques. By the time you finish this program, you will have a PHD in memory training.

I want to begin this program with a challenge for you. Over the past few years, I have made some observations of people after they purchased a book or invested in a workshop. The average investment for our live workshop is over $250 per person, and what is unbelievable to me, is that one in five of the people who enroll never attend the class after making the investment. They invest over $250, and then never attend. As incredible as that may sound, I know that the average person that invests in a program of any nature, whether it be memory training, sales, public speaking, or something else, never completes the program. I know countless individuals whose libraries are filled with courses never completed. My challenge to you is this - Complete this course! When you do, you will have learned an invaluable training.

Over the past several years, I've used this training to give speeches or presentations that lasted several hours and never accessed a single note. I've been in an elevator and recalled the name of a man I met a year and a half before for five minutes in a business environment. That simple act of recalling his name made him feel significant, and turned into a great business contact for me. It is not exciting that I have done these things. What is exciting, however, is that anyone who completes this course can do these things.

Are you ready to begin? Are you excited? I know I am. It is an important that you are willing to accept change.

The stages a person goes through when they encounter a positive change are:

1.) The first stage is typically rejection. We are creatures of habit, and anything new is often scoffed at.

2.) The next stage is when a person may see how others can use it. You might say, "Well, Ronnie, I can see how this program has worked for you, and I can see how my kids and especially my spouse could use it, but it's not for me."

3.) Then as the walls of resistance begin to crumble, you say, "I think I'll try it on a limited basis."

4.) The final stage is, "How did I ever get along without it?"

Do you remember going through these stages with the microwave oven? I do. At first you thought, "No way. Why would I use that? What is the purpose? The good old oven was good enough for my parents, and it's good enough for me. If it doesn't say 'simmer', then we're not going to use it." At the next stage, you will say, "Well, I can see how my kids might use it for a quick snack," then gradually you'll say, "Maybe I can use it every now and then to warm up leftovers." Finally, what happens, "How did I get along without it?" What percentages of meals do you at least use a microwave for a couple of things? I bet a lot. That is the fourth level of change. We accept change slowly. That is not always a bad thing. It is good to be cautious and ease into new things. However, too cautious and too slow is dangerous.

If you decide to fish, fine. If you decide to cut bait, fine. But if you do nothing, nobody eats. I ran into a woman at the Dallas/Fort Worth Airport who had attended my seminar. I said, "Colleen, how are you?" She jumped and she was so impressed that I remembered her name. I said, "Why are you impressed? You came to the workshop. You know what I'm doing. Sure it's been eight months since I met you along with a hundred other people, but you can do that, too, Colleen, you know the system." She said, "Yes," she knows the system, and she thinks it's great, but she hasn't used it to the extent she should have.

Every single person who takes this course will fall into one of two categories.

1.) They see value in the system and implement it into their daily lives whether it is slowly or all at once.

2.) They see value in the system, but because of the change that is required, fall back on the old method of no memory system.

Right now, I want you to decide which category that you are going to be in. Give the system the benefit of the doubt right now since you haven't actually learned the techniques. Tell yourself that you are not going to oppose this change and see yourself recalling names, faces, numbers, and giving speeches without notes. In every aspect of life, not just memory training, there are comfort zones. It is hard to perform outside of the comfort zones. We get used to a way of doing things and it is hard to change. A headline out of a local Seattle paper

7

a few years ago, read, "Justice Grinds Slow, Man Wants Back In Jail". He was released from a penitentiary and found his eight weeks of freedom to be terrifying, according to the newspaper. Most of us would find eight weeks in a penitentiary terrifying. Why would eight weeks on the streets be terrifying to this man? It was terrifying because he was outside of his self-image comfort zone.

What happens when we are out of our comfort zone? We have a tendency to get back where we belong, don't we? Even though that is far short of what our potential could be. This man robbed a bank in Portland, Oregon and waited to be caught. He appeared before the judge without any legal counsel. He said, "Why do I need counsel? I'm a 10-time looser". He said, "I would appreciate it if you forgo the pre-sentence investigation so that I could get back home tomorrow." Home, in the article, he says, "I want to go home."

Where is that in your life? What is the imaginary ceiling in your life? Folks, change is tough. Hopefully, no one reading this book will ever experience this situation. However, I see people do this to different degrees every day. They are comfortable with the way they are doing things and the change is scary, even if it is best for them. It could be a diet, exercise, learning a foreign language, moving to a new town, going to a new school or learning a method to recall information. Don't sell yourself short. Give yourself some credit. You have taken the action step to obtain this information and now you are reading it. Don't stop here. Let me repeat that, don't stop here.

What you are about to learn is over 2,500 years old. Can you believe that? These techniques have been around that long! In 477 BC, a Greek poet amazed everyone with his great memory. The story goes that he was at a banquet when the roof of a building fell in and killed many of those attending. The bodies had to be identified, but they were crushed beyond recognition. Simonedes came to the rescue. He was able to recall the names of everyone and where they sat. Simonedes claimed he did this by imagining the people in their places at the table during the banquet. Subsequently, a method of recalling information was derived in part from this experience.

The Greeks developed a form of memory training called Loci. It is a Latin word and it means "places". We will go into more detail on specifically how this method works and how it can work for you today. In 1959, there was another breakthrough in the area of memory. A brain surgeon, Wilder Penfield, conducted some remarkable experiments on epileptic patients. Penfield found that when he touched parts of the patient's brain with the weak electronic stimulation, the fully-conscious patient would begin talking, shouting and would begin describing memories from years past, as if reliving the experience all over again. This demonstration proved that individual memories take up residence in different parts of the brain. Similarly, different portions of the brain form different functions. For example, the left side of your brain handles language skills. People who have suffered brain damage in a particular area might have great difficulty learning abstract concepts, but can play the piano or hit a baseball as well as they ever did. The tissues of your brain share something with the rest of the body. The better you treat it through nutrition, avoiding substance abuse, and maintaining a good physical condition, the better it will work for you. Your brain is so wonderful and complex that no accident could have been its origin. It has been said that if your mind were simple enough to understand, you would be so simple that you couldn't understand it. So enjoy the 2,500 year old techniques that you are about to learn and remember, you are the greatest computer ever created.

day 2

Basic Association

Let's progress together to the next level of memory skills. I want to begin with some mental gymnastics to get your mind stimulated. Clear your mind of everything. Ok. Now, pick a number between one and ten. You got it? (Any number between one and ten). Now, multiply that number by nine. You should have a new number now. Now take the digits in the new number and add them together. For example, if your new number is 12, add one plus two and you get three. So pick a number between one and ten, multiply it by nine, and add the digits together. Now, take that new number and subtract five from it. Got it? If not, back up and get it. Now assign that number a letter of the alphabet. For example, if it's one, it is A, two is B, three is C, four is D, five is E, six is F, seven is G, eight is H, nine is I, and so on.

Now think of a country that starts with that letter. Think of a country that starts with the letter you just picked. Now go to the second letter in the name of that country and think of an animal that starts with that letter. Pick a normal color for that animal. Now, how many of you in here are thinking of a gray elephant from Denmark? Wow, huh? Can I read your mind? Hardly, I just played a simple game with you and regardless of the number chosen, 90% will end up with Denmark. It's a fun game that you can play with your friends. I wanted to do that demonstration for two reasons. Number one, I wanted to get your mind stimulated before we dive right in. Number two, I wanted to illustrate a point. What I just did was a game that you can play with your friends. That is the extent of the application of that brain teaser. What you are going to learn in this system is just as fun to do with your friends as a game. However, please do not see that as the application for this system.

Recently, I ran into a guy who had taken our live training while I was out to dinner. I said, "Hey, Ken, have you used the memory system? " He said, "Yeah, I won $100 off a friend of mine who didn't believe that I could memorize a list of 40 items after hearing it once, forwards, backwards, and by number. " We both laughed. However, I hope Ken understands the application for this system is to recall product knowledge, give speeches without notes, and remember customer names, remembering to call important clients, recalling key points to a selling presentation or helping students study. Please practice by doing demonstrations with your friends. It is fun and good practice. But, don't see this system as simply a game. If you do, you are cheating yourself. And, I wouldn't bet your friends $100 either. They probably won't be your friends much longer. Come to think of it, when I ran into Ken, he was eating alone. So, let's have some fun. Let's learn and remember that this system is going to help us in every aspect of our life.

When you decided to take action and invest in this training, you probably had just heard me on the radio or TV doing a memory demonstration. Or perhaps, this training was given to you by a close friend or business associate who told you about the demonstration that I did. Maybe, I had someone call off 15 or 20 items rapid fire, and then I repeated the list forwards and backwards. I'm going to do that same activity right now, only I am going to give YOU a list of 20 items and YOU are going to recall them. Use whatever memory system that you normally use. This is just simply a test to give us a starting point. So sit back, relax, clear your mind of all thoughts, and remember, don't write this information down. This is a memory test. I'm going to give you 20 items. Focus and get ready. I want you to memorize this list in this EXACT order. The rules are only go through this list ONCE and spend no more than five to seven seconds on each item.

1.) Pencil

2.) Sink

3.) Circus

4.) Track

5.) Star

6.) Buller

7.) Dice

8.) Hourglass

9.) Baseball

10.) Fingers

11.) Goal Post

12.) Eggs

13.) Flag

14.) Necklace

15.) Paycheck

16.) Car

17.) Magazine

18.) Soldier

19.) Golf Clubs

20.) Shot Gun

Now, get a sheet of paper and write down how many that you recall. And, yes, they do have to be with the right number and in the correct order. For instance, if I knew all seven digits in a phone number, but in the wrong order, I'd be at the phone awhile. Stop now and see how many you get.

So, how did you do? Did you get all 20? Probably not, most people get anywhere between three and five. If you got six or more, that is great! More than ten items, is definitely above average.

Now, everything done is this program is done for a purpose. We will never complete an exercise that does not have at least one application. This exercise has three applications! The first was exactly what I stated before we began. It is simply a memory test to give us a starting point, to give us a reference. In other words, I wanted you to find out what your memory capabilities were before you learn this system. So, write down how many you got correct and circle it. Did you notice anything different about this system that starts with a pencil? You may have noticed that some of the items related to the numbers. For example, number 16 was a car and you get a driver's license when you are 16. Number three was a circus, and we have all heard of a 3-ring circus. Every item on this list could actually have been associated with a number in some way. Now, I know what you're thinking. Ron, you said this system was not basic association. It's not. However, you need to have an understanding of what basic association is before we can elevate you to higher forms in memory training.

So, we are going to start with association which is first grade in terms of memory training. This pencil list, called because it starts with a pencil, is a basic association list. Let me show you what I mean.

• Number one is a pencil. The association is that the number one looks like a pencil.

• Number two is a sink. The association for 2 and sink is that it has 2 knobs, 2 options on and off, hot and cold. Someone in a workshop once said that if you look at the pipes under a sink, they kind of look like a number 2 the way they twist and bend. Now that's an imagination, but that is exactly what it takes to recall.

• Number three is a circus. The association is a 3-ring circus.

• Number four, the association is there are four lanes in a track, four times around is a mile. Remember the 4-minute mile?

• Number five is a star. What would star and number five be? If you said a star has five points, that's a good association. So, a star has five points.

• Number six is a bullet. What about this one? If you get shot by a bullet, you're six feet under, right? There are six bullets in a chamber. Six shooter.

• Number seven is dice. Seven come 11, lucky seven. Do you know that opposite sides of dice always add up to seven? Now, what was number five? Star, right, because it has five points. What about two, sink, two knobs. How about seven, dice, right? Seven come 11, opposite sides always equal seven. If there is a two on the top, the five will be on the bottom. What about number four, track, right? Four lanes, four-minute mile, four laps is one mile. Remember, this is what is called basic association. It is very basic, and all it requires is that you visualize and associate.

• Number eight is hourglass, and eight looks like an hourglass because of its shape.

• Number nine, baseball. There are nine innings, nine players on a team. Last year the Rangers blew a nine-run lead in the ninth. Now, what was two? Think about it. Sink, right? Number three, circus, right? How about seven? Dice. Seven come 11.

• Number ten is fingers. I would be willing to say that most of you have ten fingers and ten toes, so ten is fingers.

• Number 11 is a goal post. There are 11 players on each football team. When a field goal is kicked, the referee makes his arms go up like an 11. What about five? Star, right? Five points on a star. What was nine? Baseball, right? Nine innings, nine players. How about six? It was bullet. Six feet under.

• Number 12, 12 is eggs. A dozen eggs, that one is pretty easy.

• Number 13. Thirteen is a flag. What do you think the associations for 13 and flag are? Do you think of the original 13 colonies? Did you know that there are 13 stripes on our current flag? What was ten? Finger, right? Ten fingers and toes. Hold out your hands and say ten. If someone gives you five on both hands, that's ten! If you have a ten dollar bill, you wrap your fingers around it so you don't lose it.

• Number 14 is a necklace. Fourteen karat gold, Valentine's Day is February 14th. A necklace could be a Valentine's Day gift.

• Number 15 is paycheck. When do a lot of people get paid? The first and the 15th, right? Now, what if you don't get paid on the 15th? What if I told you that on the 15th of every month, I had a check for $15,000 waiting for you in my office? Would you ever forget to come by my office on the 15th? So, 15 is what, paycheck, right?

• Number 16 is a car. When do you get a driver's license? Sixteen, right?

• Number 17 is a magazine. Now, some of you men may not know that there is a magazine for teenage girls called Seventeen. So what was 17? Magazine, right? Remember, it is a magazine. How about number 14? Remember, it was necklace, 14 karat gold, Valentine's Day.

• Number 18 is a soldier. When is someone eligible for the draft? Eighteen, right?

• Nineteen is golf clubs. How many holes are on a golf course? No, not 19, there are eighteen. You golfers know that the 19th hole is where you go after the eighteenth hole to relax and have something to eat or drink.

• Number 20. Twenty is a shotgun. Twenty and shotgun. Ever heard of a 20-gauge shotgun?

Remember that this list was created using the first generation, the first level of memory training called association. It works, but very seldom. In other words, we associated nine with baseball with nine innings and nine players. If number three was baseball, that wouldn't work, would it? We couldn't use basic association because three and baseball have nothing in common. However, basic association does play a significant role in memory training and it is important to understand. What was number two? Think about it. Two knobs, the pipes look like a two, hot and cold. Sink, right?

Now I want you to get a very vivid picture in your mind of sink. Perhaps, it could be the sink in your kitchen or bathroom, that's not important. What is important is to get a clear picture in your mind. Your mind thinks in pictures. For example, clear your mind of every thought. Now, I want you to think of anything but not a dog. Don't see a dog. What happened? You thought of a dog, didn't you? What that illustrates is your mind thinks in pictures. You don't see the word, dog spelled out, you actually see a dog. Your eye is the strongest part of the memory. That is why when you see a person, you say, I recognize the face, but what is their name? That is because you saw their face. You never saw their name.

Since we know that, we recall what we see longer than what we simply hear, remember to actually visualize these items, and the bigger, the better. Make the pictures larger than life. What was seven? Seven come 11. It was dice. So, see a huge furry man-eating dice. The dice are so big that you can't even see over them. Remember, visualize huge dice. Next, what was 12? .....Eggs. A dozen eggs. Visualize 12 eggs. Maybe they are on the floor, and you're breaking them. Next, what was five?..... It has five points. Star. Good. Get a clear picture of a star with five points. What was ten?..... Fingers. Ten fingers, ten toes, holding onto a ten dollar bill. What was 14?..... Fourteen karat gold, Valentine's Day. Get a good picture of necklace in your mind. What was 17?..... Magazine. What was eight? Hourglass. What was 11?.... Goal posts. How about track?..... That was four. Four lanes, four laps. Do you remember 13? Thirteen stars, 13 stripes?

What about 15?..... Paycheck. The first and the 15th? I know that you won't forget that one.

What was number one? ...Pencil. A pencil is a straight line like a number one. Remember that this is called the pencil list because it starts with pencil.

What about number 18? Soldier. Eighteen to join the military.

What about 20?... Shotgun. Twenty-gauge shotgun.

What about 19?... That's golf clubs. Remember the 19th hole?

What about 16?... That's car. At 16, you get your driver's license.

What was number two? ... It was sink.

Number four, track, number six, bullet, number nine, baseball, number 13, flag, number 17, magazine, number 18, soldier. Remember, that this is what is called basic association. It does have its applications; however, if you try to use it for everything, you're going to be up the creek in a wire boat without a paddle.

It is time to stop and let's write down this list one more time. If you get stuck on one, skip it and go to the next one, it might come to you. Ask yourself, what was the association? Don't spend more than four or five minutes on this exercise.

Ok, how did you do? Probably a lot better than the first time for sure. Let's see, just follow along and put a check mark on the ones you got correct. Remember, they do have to be in the correct order and by the correct number.

1.) Pencil

2.) Sink

3.) Circus

4.) Track

5.) Star

6.) Buller

7.) Dice

8.) Hourglass

9.) Baseball

10.) Fingers

11.) Goal Post

12.) Eggs

13.) Flag

14.) Necklace

15.) Paycheck

16.) Car

17.) Magazine

18.) Soldier

19.) Golf Clubs

20.) Shot Gun

Did you get a better score this time? I bet you did! What we just did was an exercise in basic association. Did you get all 20? If you did, that's great! Most everyone should get at least 15 or more. If you got less than 15, the reason is that when you created the associations, the pictures were not vivid enough. Remember that your mind thinks in pictures and remembers pictures, not words or abstract thoughts. So make an effort to actually visualize everything you are attempting to recall using this system. Make your pictures huge and larger than life, the bigger the better. Don't see number seven as small dice in a Monopoly game, visualize seven-foot tall man-eating dice. I promise you that if you saw that, you would never forget it. So, see it.

You have just completed our first lesson. I know it was basic; however, you must crawl before you walk. This course will slowly elevate you through the levels of memory training until eventually you will have a Masters Degree in memory training. This is what is called basic association. When I meet people and I tell them that I teach memory training, they say, "Oh, association, I know all about that." Perhaps they do. However, memory training goes much deeper than that. Association is the first level. You have just completed Day two. I know right now you're thinking that this is too basic, and you're right, we're at a very basic stage. Association can't be used for everything. However, you must understand it before we progress to the next level. Trust me; we are starting at the first grade level. Remember when you learned how to read, you had to learn the alphabet first. Then when you got to high school, you read Shakespeare. Day two is learning the alphabet. By the time we get to Day 30, you are going to have a PHD in memory training.

day 3

Chain of Visualization

The next level of association includes elements of memory training, such as acronyms. Have you heard of acronyms? An acronym is a series of letters created using the first letter of each word. IBM is an acronym for International Business Machines. AT&T is an acronym for American Telephone and Telegraph. These are used by companies because they are easier to remember. When I was in high school, my science teacher told me that I could learn the colors of the rainbow in the correct order by remembering the name Roy G Biv.

R for red, O for orange, y for yellow, G for green, B for blue, I for indigo, and V for violet. Another acronym I learned in school was an easy way to remember the Great Lakes. It is called homes. H.O.M.E.S. H for Huron, O for Ontario, M for Michigan, E for Erie and S for Superior. That is an easy way to learn the Great Lakes.

Can acronyms be used for everything? No. Are there more advanced ways to retain information? Yes. However, every level of memory training is important, and you never know when a good old fashioned acronym is what you need to use to recall some vital information. Remember, this course is meant to be learned in levels. I'm sure that right now at this point you would love to know how to memorize a 100 digit number after only hearing it once. Believe me, we will get there. Patience is the key. You can't skip any steps. Believe it or not, we are going to use the pencil list later to learn how to count in Japanese. I know you find that hard to believe right now, but just watch. You're going to be amazed.

Have you ever heard how a bamboo tree grows? You'll water it every day for five years and see nothing. And one day in the fifth year, it will grow from several feet in a period of a few weeks. Did it grow in a few weeks or five years? It obviously grew in five years. But, the results were seen in the few weeks because of the work put in before. Your memory is the same way. Right now, we are watering it, but by the end of this program, it is going to grow very large, very quickly.

Acronyms and links are in this 'watering' stage. A link is a method of recalling information by telling a story. Many ancient books, such as the Bible, were passed down from one generation to the next this way. I bet you can sing many of your favorite tunes on the radio and not miss a beat. The reason is that you have, number one, incorporated the link method of memorizing by linking one thought to the next, songs also incorporate rhythm which helps your memory. A link is simply linking one thought to the next. For example, here is a list of 19 items. If I ask you to memorize them using basic association, it would not work. For example, number one is Mount Rainier, number two is ice, number three is trees, number four is bicycle. What do these items have in common with the number they are with? Nothing that I am aware of. So, in this case, basic association would not work.

The next level is the chain of association or the link. Sit back, relax and enjoy this story. I want you to focus on seeing the images in this story very clearly, vividly and powerfully. Here is the story:

Mount Rainier has ice on the top and trees on the side. Coming down the mountain is a bicycle ridden by a German shepherd. He has a glass of water in one hand and a shoe in the other. At the bottom of the mountain, he crashes into a TV set and lands on a pillow. He bounces off the pillow onto a trampoline, and bounces off the trampoline into an airplane. The airplane lands in Dallas and Richard Nixon is waiting for him. He has on a brown hat, black boots; he hands him a check for $50,000 and the keys to a brand new Corvette. He then drives the Corvette back to Mount Rainier.

Now, we're going to do this one more time. The difference is I want you to repeat the items out loud. By the way, if you move your hands and use body language, you'll have reinforced the pictures in your mind. So, here we go. Sit back and read this story. Mount Rainier has ice on the top and trees on the side. Repeat with me. Mount Rainier has ice on the top and trees on the side. Coming down the mountain is a bicycle ridden by a German Shepherd. Repeat with me, coming down the mountain is a bicycle ridden by a German Shepherd. He has a glass of water in one hand and a shoe in the other. Repeat with me, he has a glass of water in one hand and a shoe in the other. At the bottom of the mountain, he crashes into a TV set. Repeat with me, at the bottom of the mountain, he crashes into a TV set. He lands on a pillow, bounces on a trampoline, and bounces off the trampoline into an airplane. Repeat with me, he lands on a pillow, bounces on a trampoline, and bounces off the trampoline into an airplane. The airplane lands in Dallas and Richard Nixon is waiting for him. Repeat with me, the airplane lands in Dallas and Richard Nixon is waiting for him. He has on a brown hat and black boots. Repeat with me, he has a brown hat and black boots. He hands him a check for $50,000 and the keys to a brand new Corvette. Repeat with me, he hands him a check for $50,000 and the keys to a brand new Corvette. He then drives the Corvette back to Mount Rainier. Repeat with me, he then drives the Corvette back to Mount Rainier. Did you use body language with it? I always do. I hold out my hands like I'm holding a glass of water and a shoe. I bounce like I'm on the trampoline and I act like I'm Richard Nixon, and I stick out my hands like they have keys and $50,000 in them.

Let's do this one more time. Here we go. Focus on the story:

22

Mount Rainier has ice on the top and trees on the side. Repeat with me. Mount Rainier has ice on the top and trees on the side. Coming down the mountain is a bicycle ridden by a German Shepherd. Repeat with me. Coming down the mountain is a bicycle ridden by a German Shepherd. He has a glass of water in one hand and a shoe in the other. Repeat with me, he has a glass of water in one hand and a shoe in the other. At the bottom of the mountain, he crashes into a TV set. Repeat with me, at the bottom of the mountain, he crashes into a TV set. He lands on a pillow, bounces to a trampoline, and bounces off the trampoline into an airplane. Repeat with me, he lands on a pillow, bounces to a trampoline, and then bounces off the trampoline into an airplane. The airplane lands in Dallas and Richard Nixon is waiting for him. Repeat with me, the airplane lands in Dallas and Richard Nixon is waiting for him. He has a brown hat and black boots. Repeat with me, he has a brown hat and black boots. He hands him a check for $50,000 and the keys to a brand new Corvette. Repeat with me, he hands him a check for $50,000 and the keys to a brand new Corvette. He then drives the Corvette back to Mount Rainier. Repeat with me, he then drives the Corvette back to Mount Rainier.

Now it is time to see how many that you recalled. Now, on a sheet of paper write down all the items in this list. Don't write out the story, instead, simply write each noun in the story. For example, Mount Rainier will be the first item on the list.

Set the book aside now and write down the items there are 16 items. Do not spend more than four to five minutes on this exercise. After you done come back and check your answers. Answers below:

1.) Mount Rainier

2.) Bicycle

3.) German Shepherd

4.) Glass of water

5.) Shoe

6.) TV set

7.) Pillow

8.) Trampoline

9.) Airplane

10.) Dallas

11.) Richard Nixon

12.) Brown hat

13.) Black boots

14.) check for $50,000

15.) Keys to a brand new Corvette

16.) Mount Rainier

Well, how did you do? Did the link method work for you? I bet you did pretty well. Our minds are truly the greatest computers ever created, and I mean that. Don't get caught up in being perfect right now. Just make sure that you understand the concepts before we progress to the next level. Remember that this course is a building block process. Make sure you understand basic association, acronyms, and the link method before you move on.

day 4

A 2000 Year Old Memory Method

Radio certainly has entertained millions over the years and the great radio programs of the 30's, 40's and 50's are classics. What an experience that must have been, sitting by the radio creating your own pictures of the stories that were being told. I bet everyone listening had different images of the characters. What they looked like, what they wore, what their families looked like. That is the beauty of the imagination and the power of the mind. I am a huge Texas Rangers baseball fan. I can remember listening to the Ranger games on the radio late at night when I was 12 and 13. I can remember the pictures I created in my head. I remember visualizing the baseball and the sounds of the crowd that evoked the pictures and emotions that I felt when I was actually there.

Imagine this - A huge lemon is sitting on the table in front of you. Can you see it? It is the size of a grapefruit. Take your right hand and visualize yourself cutting down the middle of that lemon. See the juices oozing all over the tablecloth. Sitting on the table is two halves of the lemon. Pick up one of the lemons and hold that half up to your nose. Do you smell the lemon? Is the moisture from the lemon getting your nose wet? Now, with the hand holding the lemon against your mouth, open your mouth as wide as you can, and think of the meat of that lemon in your mouth. Bite down on the lemon and let the juices drip down your face.

Did you salivate? Did your face squish up into a bitter expression? The next question you should be asking yourself is why did I make those expressions? What provoked them? Your mind thinks in pictures and often it cannot tell the difference between an actual picture or a picture that exists in your mind only. Your mind truly is incredible. That is why athletes visualize their successes or their golf swings, or batting swings, catching footballs long before they actually do those things, because their minds believe that it is real. If the visualization is strong enough, then you are actually conditioning your mind for success with pictures. Your mind utilizes pictures to retain information and we are going to use that knowledge to our benefit. Pay close attention to next few thoughts. They are going to be the nuts and bolts of this program. Everything will build on them, so this is very important. What we are about to learn is actually the system that the Romans developed 2,500 years ago.

Remember the Loci we talked about, that is the Latin word for places? The Romans actually developed places in their minds where they would store information. They discovered that your mind actually works like a filing system. Here's a modern day example. Most of us use computers in some fashion. It is hard to get by without one. When you have information you wish to keep, what do you do? You store it on a disk, a CD, print it and file it. Let me create a picture that might be a horror story for some of you who work with computers.

Let's say a hacker got into your computer and deleted all the directories, files and program titles. Everything was still in your computer hard drive, but it was no longer labeled. Wouldn't that be a mess? The information would still be in there, but finding it would be a big problem. The analogy is this: everything you have ever seen, heard, or done is still in your memory. Accessing and retrieving it is the difficulty. Many students have told me that when they are taking a test, they know the information but they don't remember it until the test is over a few hours later. They knew it; they just couldn't get the information out of their memories when they needed it. This will happen with business professionals when they leave out a part of their presentation and then recall it when the meeting is over. The stress is off and your mind throws it up. However, it is obviously too late then. So, just like the computer, the information is in there. Finding it when you need it is the difficulty. The system the Romans developed, allows you to create files and directories in your mind and store information in those files. Sounds pretty cool, doesn't it? Well, guess what? It is.....it's very cool. It has transformed my life.

Remember, I told you to listen closely, because the next part will be the nuts and bolts of memory training. Well, here it is. The Romans discovered that you need five things to recall anything... numbers, poems, scripture, dates, presentations or names. The items are the same your computer uses.

1.) Focus
2.) Location
3.) Code
4.) Action
5.) Review

The first item of business is focus. You must consciously focus your memory. There are many supplements that you can take to focus your memory and one of my favorites is Omega-3 Fish Oil pills. In addition to this, supplement that includes ingredients is going to be great for

---

Foods good for memory:

Spinach	Blueberries	Red onions
Apples	Red Beets	Grapes
Cherries	Eggplant	Rosemary

---

your memory and ability to focus. You will be able to find this naturally in some foods such spinach and blueberries as well.

Next, when you store information on your computer, where do you put it? You put it in a file or directory to retrieve it later. Your mind works the same way. The code your memory recognizes is pictures, so we turn everything we want to recall into a picture. That is the code our mind thinks in. Number four, that item is action. What holds the code in the file on the computer? The circuits hold the information in a storage unit until it is deleted. Action is the circuit for our memories. That may not make sense right now, but it will as we progress. So you may be saying to yourself, "Great, Ron, but what is a place where I can mentally store information?" I don't have circuits in my head. Believe it or not, you do.

As Wilder Penfield discovered in 1959, you actually have items in your mind right now that are files, and you don't even know it. Can you believe that? It's true. Here are some questions about the town that you live in. Can you visualize the school? What about the fire department, your home, the police station, maybe a public swimming pool, a river, the park, a hotel, a car dealership or a restaurant. Could you visualize those things? I bet you could. They are there. They exist. These are what the Romans called files. What the Romans would do is start at the north end of their town and then chose an item like a park, or a river, or a stadium, or a tree, or an object that stood out, and that would be their first file. As they moved south through the town, they would choose items in a very systematic north to south method until they had maybe 25 or 30 files. Some probably had many more files. Your town could actually be a file system.

I had the good fortune to live in downtown Seattle in my twenties and I took a job as a waiter. On one of my first days there, I was asked to learn the food menu. Did I use this opportunity to spotlight my memory? Sure I did. A little showing off is good every now and then.

What I did was pick buildings around Seattle as my files. The space needle was my number one file. The King Dome was number two. Safeco Field was number three, and other restaurants and buildings were my files until I had about 20. I even used the bay and some of the piers. Remember, the next step in recalling information is to turn it into a code that your mind remembers, and that code is what? The code our minds remember with is pictures. So, I turned the menu items into pictures and filed them with action. What is action, you ask? Good question, but wait just a minute before we get to that part.

Remember, you are a bamboo tree. I impressed everyone with how easy I was able to do this using my newly created city files. I started conversations and I even taught people I worked with how to do it. It even helped me make friends. You didn't know this course could do that, did you? Pretty cool, huh? So right now you should be getting a general idea how this system works, but not exactly. Right now you may be thinking, "This sounds fascinating!" But perhaps you don't see exactly how it works so the application. If that is how you are thinking, then good. That's exactly where you should be. If you were supposed to understand everything right now, we would stop the program here. We aren't going to do that.

In a moment you are going to draw out your own 'City Files'. What you need to do is visualize your town from a bird's eye view. The top of the page is the North, and pick ten items that you can use as files. Remember, good files are buildings, restaurants, schools, houses or even a gas station. Now, do this in a systematic way. Work north to south or east to west, or even clockwise, just make it logical. As you draw a box or diagram to denote the file, place a number beside it, one through ten.

Here is an example of what your city files might look like:

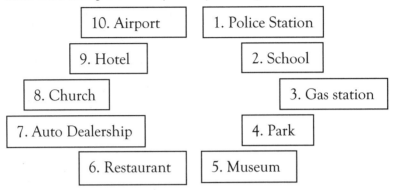

10. Airport   1. Police Station

9. Hotel   2. School

8. Church   3. Gas station

7. Auto Dealership   4. Park

6. Restaurant   5. Museum

Once again, pick ten files in your city; write them down and memorize them!

How did you do? Did you zip right through it? You have just created your first ten files. It should be kind of exciting. Now, let's not beat around the bush any longer, let's use them. I'm going to give you ten pictures, and we are going to file them to you ten city files. Again, what are the five things you need to recall anything?

1.) Focus

2.) Location

3.) Code

4.) Action

5.) Review

Before we dive right in, let me ask you a few questions. Can you remember every time you've gotten in a car and driven somewhere? Most of us can't. But I bet you can tell me the time you were driving and someone pulled out in front of you and your cars collided. You could probably tell me the time of day, where you were going, what you were driving, and what they were driving. Now, the question is, why? What is the difference? That picture was vivid and it had emotions tied to it. I bet you can't tell me every time you have gone to see a movie or had dinner with someone, but what about that first date or the first break up? Those are things that have emotion tied to them and are stronger in our memories. So, the number four in our system is the action, and that is what we use to create the vivid picture with the emotion tied to it. The more vivid and emotional the action is, the better you will recall it. Just like the lemon analogy. It has to be vivid.

By now your city files need to be driven into your memory and you need to know them forwards and backwards. Below you will find a list of ten words. Using the city files that you created place each of these objects mentally on your location and visualize it with action. If the first word you want to memorize is water then see a giant glass of water pouring out onto your location. Remember the more vivid and larger than life your image the better chance that you will recall it.

So here is the list. Scan through it as quickly as possible and use your locations on your city files, imagine larger than life images and here we go:

1.) Photo Album

2.) Igloo

3.) Cactus

4.) Noah's Ark

5.) Gold bars

6.) The color red

7.) Doctor stitching a cut

8.) Clothes made of dollar bills

9.) Oranges

10.) Peaches

Now write down the ten pictures to test your recall. Don't write the file or the action down, just the picture. For example, number one, just write photo album. If you get stuck on one, don't worry about it. Don't get bogged down on one item. You can always come back to it later. Ask yourself, what was your file and then the picture should come to you.   When you complete this test, come back to the program.

So, how did you do? Did you get all ten of them? If you did, pat yourself on the back.   That is a great accomplishment. Remember, when you heard about this memory system, and you heard that I was able to hear items once and then recall them forwards, backwards, or by number, you were impressed. You were not impressed with the process; you were impressed with the results. Once, a lady who attended one of our live classes in Dallas was disappointed because our system was so simple. I explained to her that's not a drawback. That is the beauty of this system. I have read every study and program done on memory training. I could make this course difficult and cumbersome. But why would I want to do that when you can

> *First 10 States in*
> *Alphabetical Order:*
>
> 1.) *Alabama*
>
> 2.) *Alaska*
>
> 3.) *Arizona*
>
> 4.) *Arkansas*
>
> 5.) *California*
>
> 6.) *Colorado*
>
> 7.) *Connecticut*
>
> 8.) *Delaware*
>
> 9.) *Georgia*
>
> 10.) *Florida*

get phenomenal results with such a simple process?

Now, how many did you get right? If you got nine or ten, pat yourself on the back. If you got eight or less, ask yourself why. It can only be one of two reasons. Either, number one you did not know your file, or number two your picture wasn't vivid enough. If you knew your file, but you missed it, it's because the picture wasn't strong enough. Make sure that you know your files by heart and that the pictures that you create are vivid. By the way, did you know that I just taught you a list that actually means something and you didn't even know it? Often times to recall something, we are going to have to turn an abstract into a picture. That is exactly what we just did. We turned ten abstract words into pictures, and I filed them to our files. Would you believe me that if I just told you just learned the first ten states of the United States in alphabetical order? Well, guess what? You did.

Remember, each state is an abstract word. We used a picture or something we could represent to see it. Let's see what I mean. What was number one? ..... Photo album. The first state in alphabetical order is Alabama. A photo album for Alabama. Number two is igloo. What do you think that represents? Alaska, right? Number three, cactus. Did you guess Arizona? If you did you're right. Number four, Noah's Ark. Almost too easy. Arkansas. Number five, gold bars. Where was the gold rush in 1849? California, of course. Number six, the color red. How about Colorado? Number seven, stitching a cut? What are you doing? You are connecting a cut.... Connecticut. Connecting-a-cut. Number eight, dollar bill wear. Delaware. Dollar bill wear, Delaware. Number nine, oranges. What state is known for oranges? Florida, of course. Number ten, peaches. How about Georgia? There you have it! The first ten states in alphabetical order. Did you think it was going to be that easy? You have learned quite a bit today. Stop and pick up tomorrow on Day five.

day 5

Skeleton Files

Are you ready to dig in and expand your memory? Let's review what we have learned on Day four. To recall something, you must have five things. They are focus, a location, a code, an action and review. A location or a file is simply a place to store information. It could be anything at all. For example, the first building in your city files is your number one file. All ten of the files work together in this filing system. Anything can be a file system as long as it goes in a logical order and you can see or visualize each item. For example, your car could be a file system with ten files. These could be your car files. Number one is your front bumper, number two is your hood or engine, number three is your front windshield, number four is your steering wheel, number five is your gear shift, number six could be your glove box, seven could be your passenger seat, eight could be the back seat, nine could be the trunk and number ten is your license plate. Remember, you don't have to use these as one of your filing systems, but you certainly can. They are wonderful to use.

The reason, however, I wanted to bring them up is to illustrate that anything can be a file system. Your favorite golf course could be an 18-file system. Maybe one of those holes has a sand trap or water hazard next to it. Well, that would be your file for that one. The Ballpark in Arlington where the Texas Rangers play is a file system for me. Number one is the pitcher's mound, number two is home plate, number three is first base, number four is second and so on. Ok, do you get the idea? We are going to create a file system that I think you're going to like. It's kind of fun.

There are ten files in this system, and it is called our skeleton files. Why? Because the files are you! You are a file system. I bet you can visualize this. It is important to verbalize and touch your files. These are going to be permanent files for you, and you must call them what I call them. The reason will make sense later. This may be the most important file system you have learned up to this point. So, are you ready for your next ten files? Here we go! Number one is the top of your head. We are going to call it top. So, say top and touch the top of your head. I know that you may feel silly. You may say, "Ron, this is silly." Do you think so? Well, I will tell you what is silly, forgetting to call a client because you fail to remember, or giving a speech and forgetting what you are supposed to say. That, my friends, is silly.

This system is a little different, but have fun with it. So again, what was number one? It was the top of your head. So, say top and pat the top of your head. Your number two file is going to be your nose, so pat your nose and say number two. What was your one? One was top. What was number two? Two is nose. Your number three file is your mouth. Say mouth and then touch your mouth. What was one? Top. Two was nose, and three is mouth. Notice we're just moving from top to bottom. Your number four file is your ribs. So, grab your ribs and hold onto them and say number four is my ribs. What is number four? It is your ribs. Your fifth file is your liver. It is right in the lower half of your torso. We are halfway through.

Number six is going to be your hip joint. We are going to call it joint. So, touch your number six file and say number six is my joint. What is four? Ribs, right? What about number one? Top. What about four? Ribs. What was number six? Joint. Ok, our number seven file is going to be your knee cap. We are just going to call it cap.

So, seven is cap. What is seven? Cap. Pat it and say number seven is cap. What about five? How about liver? What was three? Mouth. What about number one? It was top.

Our number eight file is going to be a bone in our lower leg. There are two bones in your lower leg between your knee cap and ankle. One of them is your fibula. So, repeat after me. Number eight is fibula. Touch your leg and repeat. Number eight is fibula. Number nine is on the very bottom. It is the ball of your foot. We are going to call it ball. So, what is number nine? It is ball. Number seven, it is cap. Number five, liver. Number four, ribs, number six, joint. And number ten is not on your skeleton. It is actually the ground. We are going to call it the sand. So, point to the ground or the floor and say number ten is the sand.

Let's review real quick. Number one is top, two is nose, three is mouth, four is ribs, five is liver, six is joint, seven is cap, eight is fibula, nine is ball and ten is sand. These are your ten skeleton files, and it is very important that you know them. Stop and repeat each file. Here is a diagram now memorize it!

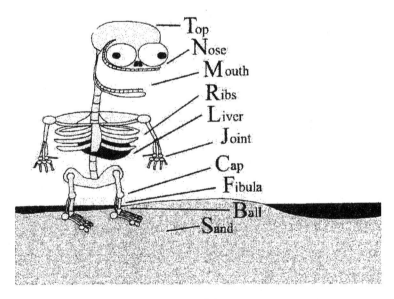

So how did you do? Pretty simple, right? You betcha! That is the beauty of this system. Later, believe it or not, the skeleton files are going to be instrumental in learning how to recall long digit numbers or phone numbers. Now, we are going to go through the same process as we did the city files. I am going to give you a list of words and you are going to memorize them using your body as the location storage. If you need to stop and make sure that you know your skeleton files then do that before proceeding. Are you ready? Clear your mind of all distractions.

Here is a list of ten items and file the first one to your first skeleton file and the second one to your second file and so on. Move as fast as you can through this list. Don't wait until you are 100% certain that you have the image mentally glued. Force yourself to go faster than you think is doable and you will be amazed with your recall. However, keep it in perspective the speed is not the crucial ingredient at this stage...understanding the system is the focus.

1.) Speaker
2.) Gun
3.) Soldier
4.) Spotlight
5.) A picture of you

Bill of Rights

1. Freedom of speech

2. Right to Bear Arms

3. Protection From Quartering Troops

4. Freedom from Unreasonable Search and Seizure

5. Right to not self-incriminate

6. Right to Speedy Trial

7. Right to Trial by Jury

8. Prohibition of excessive bail

9. Protection of Rights Not Enumerated

10. Protection of State's Rights

6.) Judge riding a fast motorcycle

7.) Jury

8.) Excessive amount of money

9.) Making a right turn with your hand over your mouth

10.) State Capitol building

Review all ten very quickly and attach them to your files as rapidly as you can. Do not take more than one minute on this at most. Now, write down the ten pictures we just filed. Rejoin the program when you complete this process.

So, how did you do? Did you get all ten? If not, ask yourself why. It is for one of two reasons. Either number one, you didn't know your file, or number two, your picture wasn't vivid enough. There is no other option. Remember, in order to recall something, you must turn an abstract into a picture. We just filed the first ten amendments to the Constitution, the Bill of Rights, to our skeleton files. Did you believe that we could do that? We did. Many students spend all day saying the Bill of Rights over and over. You just learned it forwards, backwards, and by number in less than five minutes. You don't believe me? Let's see.

Number one was speaker. Well, speaker stands for freedom of speech. Number two, what did we file to the nose? A gun, right? That amendment says we have the right to bear arms. Number three. What was three? Soldier. No soldier shall be quartered in a house without the consent of the owner. Number four, a search light. You had a search light on your ribs. Freedom from unreasonable search and seizure. Number five, you had a picture of yourself in your liver, didn't you? No one will be called to testify against themselves. Number six, was a judge riding a fast motorcycle. Remember, right there on your joint, you had a judge riding a fast motorcycle? That was an abstract to a speedy trial. Number seven. What was it? A jury of 12. That picture representative of the right to a trial by jury. Number eight is an excessive amount of money. Remember, we had an excessive amount of money coming out of our fibula? That amendment is that there shall be no excessive bail. Number nine. What did we file to the ball of our foot? We filed you making a right hand turn with your hand over your mouth. This amendment says that person's may have rights even if they are not mentioned in the constitution (hand over mouth for not mentioned) and these rights can still be violated. Number ten is a state capitol, right? We had a state capitol on the sand? That amendment talked about state's rights.

Now, I think that you will agree that these pictures were somewhat unusual. When you are doing this on your own, you're going to have the freedom to make your own pictures. If you are a student, this example in application should be very obvious to you. If you're a business professional, I hope you can also see the application. The skeleton file could be used to recall a "things to do list," steps in a presentation, procedures, organization mission statements or to give a speech. The applications are endless. Each day, I am going to use generic examples, but please be creative. This system can truly change the way you go about your daily life if you let it. I encourage you to do that.

day 6

Pencil List Practice

Welcome back. It's now Day six. Can you feel your memory expanding? I hope that this process is exciting for you. The system you are learning is just that. This is a very specific system that business professionals and students from around the country, and for that matter, the world, are using to impact their lives. Now, let's review. What are the five things you need to memorize anything? Number one focus, next a location or a file, number three is a code, which is the picture and number

> 1.) Focus
>
> 2.) Location
>
> 3.) Code
>
> 4.) Action
>
> 5.) Review

four is action and five is review. And, remember, a file can be anything. It is simply a place in your mind that you can see or visualize. A file is a building in your city or your nose, your mouth or even a hole on your favorite golf course. It is also important to recall that each file system has more than one file. For example, your skeleton files, you have top, nose, mouth, and so on. Each one of them is a file. However, when placed together, they are a file system. As long as there is more than one of them, they go in a logical order, and you can see them, they can be used as a file system. Remember, the only limit is your imagination. The code, as you recall, is the picture.

Computers translate everything they store to a code so they can recall it later. The computer between your ears works exactly the same way, and the code that your mind recalls is pictures. Your mind remembers pictures that are unusual and have emotion tied to them. And if you are missing some items when we go back and review our list, it is for one of two reasons. Either you did not know your file, or if you knew your file but did not know your information, the reason is the picture you created was not vivid enough. The circuit board in your memory is the glue that you create.

You have ten skeleton files and ten city files. We learned the pencil list and we learned how to use acronyms and link method. These are all valid forms of memory training. We are going to cover giving speeches without notes, learning poems or scripture, product knowledge, things to do list, math formulas, foreign languages and much more. Let's review our pencil list:

1.) Pencil	11. Goal Post
2.) Sink	12. Eggs
3.) Circus	13. Flag
4.) Track	14. Ring
5.) Star	15. Paycheck
6.) Bullet	16. Car
7.) Dice	17. Magazine
8.) Hour Glass	18. Soldier
9.) Baseball	19. Golf Clubs
10.) Fingers	20. Shot Gun

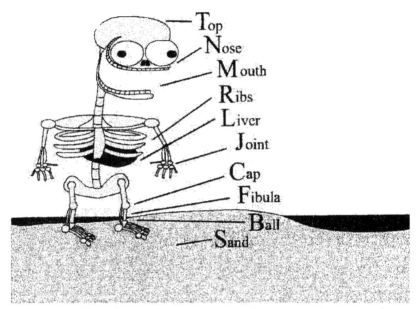

These are files, places where we store information. Knowing these are going to be crucial for recalling numbers. Perhaps you have heard or seen me do the demonstration where someone will give me a 100 digit number, and I will recall it forwards, backwards, and by the number it was call out at. I did this, believe it or not, building up on the concepts we learned in the skeleton files. So everything we have learned up to this point is crucial and has a purpose.

The activities for today are simply to go back and read the activities we have completed each day and make sure you understand the lessons in each.

day 7

Counting in Japanese

You have learned a lot so far, but the fun is just beginning. As you will recall, anything can be a file system as long as there is more than one and it goes in a logical order, and it is something that you can use. Since these are the qualifications, our pencil list is actually going to be a file system for you just like the skeleton files and the city files are. So, let's review the first ten files on our pencil list. I chose to use the word file because that is exactly what they are going to be. Places where we can store information. It could be lines of a poem or scripture, or as you will see later, we are going to learn a quote by Teddy Roosevelt very soon. Remember, that your mind thinks in pictures, and you must see these files in order to recall them.

Don't get bored that we are reviewing this file system again. I know that it may seem redundant, and at this point, I'll grant you, it is, but please take my word for it, that at this point is very necessary. We will get less and less redundant as we go and you become more comfortable with this system. But, don't give up now. You've invested too much time and this is going to pay off in a big way for you. You will see what I mean as we go.

Number one, what is our file? It is a pencil. So get a clear picture in your mind of a pencil. Perhaps, it is a pencil holder on your desk, or a pencil sharpener, or a giant man-eating pencil with arms and legs. It doesn't matter what you see. The only stipulation is that you see a clear picture of a pencil and it always is the same image that you are going to use for this file. For example, my number one file is a pencil holder on my desk.

Number two, what is your file? It's a sink. Get a very clear picture in your mind of a sink. It could be a kitchen sink, or a bathroom sink or a sink at your office. It doesn't matter, just see it, and just make sure you always use the same one.

Number three, what is your file? It's circus. Get an image of a circus in your mind. What do you think of when you think of circus? Is it the tent, the elephants, the trapeze artists? Just see a circus and always use that image as your file.

Number four, what's your file? It's track.. It could be a professional track at the Olympics, or a high school, or a college track or even a track for race cars. Just make sure every time you use the same track.

Number five, what is our file? It's star. What do you think of when I say star? Is it the star on a flag, or maybe a night sky with the stars in the sky? Just see it.

Number six, what is your file? It's bullet. Visualize the Lone Ranger's silver mullet or an M16 it doesn't matter. Just have a clear bullet in your mind's eye.

Number seven, what is your file? It is dice. Get an image of dice. Maybe it is a Monopoly board, or a craps table or another game. Just make sure it is always the same picture for dice.

Number eight, what is your file? It's an hourglass. Get an image in your head. Maybe you have an hourglass on your table or desk. Once a man said he sees his wife, because she has an hourglass figure. Whatever you see, it doesn't matter, just be consistent.

Number nine, what is your file? It is baseball. It could be a baseball player, a bat, a ball, a glove, a stadium...it doesn't matter. Just make it a clear picture and always use that image for your file.

Number ten, what is your file? It's fingers, Now, this one will be pretty easy. It's familiar for all of us. Get an image of a hand in your mind.

We're going to stop there, but go back and review 11 through 20 when we wrap up for today and make sure you have pictures for all those numbers. Now, I am going to give you ten pictures, and you are going to file these ten pictures to your first ten pencil list files. The files will be the pencil list and below are the ten words. Remember move as fast as possible and test how fast you can memorize this list in the correct order.

1.) Itching

2.) Knee

3.) Sun

4.) Girl

5.) Green traffic light

6.) Fonzi (from 'Happy Days') in a row boat

7.) The Sea and cheese (two word on this one)

8.) Queso dip (hot melted cheese)

9.) Fonzi

10.) Chew

Okay, now write down these ten words in this exact order.

So, how did you do? Did you get a perfect score? If you did, give yourself a pat on the back. Now, if you didn't, ask yourself why? Did you know your file for each one? If you knew your file, and you were still unable to recall the information, it is because your picture was not vivid enough. Create a very strong image in your mind. If you see it, you will most likely not forget it. Now, before we wrap up our lesson for the day, what do you think that we just learned? We just learned to count to ten in Japanese!

one	ichi
two	ni
three	san
four	shi
five	go
six	roku
seven	shichi
eight	hachi
nine	kyu
ten	ju

1.) Itching = Ichi
2.) Knee = Ni
3.) Sun = San
4.) Girl = Shi (the pronoun she)
5.) Green Traffic Light = Go
6.) Fonzi in a row boat = Roku (ku is pronounced like cool and no one is cooler than Fonzi!)
7.) Sea and cheese = Shichi
8.) Hot cheese = Hachi
9.) Fonzi = Ku (cool)
10.) Chew = Ju

You can now count in Japanese! You may think that well, big deal, that was easy to learn! And you're right, it was. However, it was easy because we approached it from the correct angle the first time.

If you are a student who had to learn how to count in Japanese in less than seven minutes, forwards and backwards, and by number, and you didn't have a memory system, I think that you would find it a daunting task. It was simple because of the system we used. However, as simple as it is, it is effective. Today, you learned a lot. It was a full lesson. So, take it in and pat yourself on the back for completing the lesson!

day 8

Memorizing Math Formulas

We're almost done building files. We are not going to review our skeleton files anymore. You have them at this point. If you don't, stop and make sure that you do. Before we begin filing anything to our body files, let me tell you two quick stories. Don't file these stories to files, just visualize them.

This is your first story: You have a huge globe in front of you. It is a 6-foot tall globe. As you stand in front of the globe, notice that there are seven continents, and some overlap into the northern and southern hemisphere, but the majority of them are in the north. There are four in the northern hemisphere and three in the southern hemisphere. So, let's review. What is in front of you? A globe. How many continents in the north? Four. In the south? Three. Now, you notice a piece of a pie on top of the globe and you reach up to grab a piece of the pie, but just as soon as you do, you see a rat has been eating the pie, and you don't want to eat after a rat. He's at the North Pole, so he's frozen or an ice cube. Right? Now, what was our picture? We had a globe, and how many continents in the north? Four. And what about the south? Three. What was on top of the globe? Pie. What was then next to the pie? A rat, and he was an ice cube. Now, move the picture off the screen of your mind. I'm going to give you a new picture.

Here is the second story : I want to introduce you to a friend of mine. He is a giant man-eating bumble bee from Texas. He is from Texas, so he is wearing a giant cowboy hat. Picture some parallel bars in your mind. This bee walks out with the hat and hops on the parallel bars and starts doing gymnastics. Now, if you saw that, you would never forget it. No. So, see it. Ok. Now, you have two stories in your mind that are actually pictures. What we did was take some abstract thoughts, and actually they were calculus formulas and we turned them into pictures and we filed them to our files. Let me show you what I mean.

A stockbroker once attended my course in Austin, Texas. He was studying for his Series seven test. He brought a book full of formulas. He had a lot of anxiety for the test. He was afraid he was not going to be able to recall the formulas. We approached them the exact way we approached these calculus formulas. What was the first story? It was about a globe, right? A globe is actually a sphere. So, the formula was to learn to volume formula for a sphere. That formula is sphere=4/3 $\bar{O}r^2$. Each one of these items is an abstract thought, so we had to turn it into a picture. A globe for sphere, four continents in the north and three in the south, for 4/3. And a pie for the math symbol representing 3.14, and a rat to represent r, and he is an ice cube to represent cubed. That's pretty easy. Each item simply has to be turned into a picture to recall it, and then we created a story just like the Mount Rainier story.

The stockbroker thought he was going to have to turn pictures for each formula and that seemed like a daunting task for him. He didn't think there was any way. However, after looking at the formulas, he realized that the same symbols appeared in each formula over and over again. So, yes, he did have to turn each symbol into a picture, but he had to do it once. The next time he saw that symbol in an equation, he already had a picture for it. In calculus, r is a symbol that appears in a lot of formulas and stands for radius. So, if you are dealing with formulas, you only have to turn the variables into a picture once, the first time. Let's review the second formula real quick. It was the area formula for a parallelogram. The formula is written this way, parallelogram = bh, which means base times height. So, we had parallel bars for parallelogram, and a bee for b, and a cowboy hat for h. Pretty simple. Parallelogram = bh.

If you are a student, the applications are obvious. If you are a business professional, a concept is actually more important than the formulas. So, make sure you understand the concept. You just learned two calculus formulas whether you wanted to or not. And, remember it didn't seem like a challenge because we approached it from the correct angle the first time. If you are a student struggling to learn $4/3 \tilde{O}r^2$, and then you were given this memory system, I think you would appreciate it much more. So, be thankful that you didn't have to go through that to get the information.

<u>Volume Formula</u>

Sphere = $4/3 \; \pi \; R^3$

<u>Area</u>

Parallelogram = BH

Circular Ring = $2 \; \pi \; PW$

When recalling formulas, you must substitute a picture for the symbol or variable.

<u>Math Symbol</u>		<u>Picture</u>
Sphere	=	Globe
π (pi)	=	Piece of Pie
R (radius)	=	Rat
Parallelogram	=	Parallel Bars
B (base)	=	Bumble bee
H (height)	=	Hat
Circular Ring	=	Ring

P (perimeter)	=	Pirate
W (width)	=	Window

day 9

Creating Your House Files

What we are about to do is create some new files. These are my favorite files, and this is my favorite filing system. I love them. I use this file system 90% of the time. So, what is it? It's called house files. We're going to use our homes as filing systems. It is very similar to the city files, the only difference that instead of landmarks around our city, we are using rooms or areas of our house. This system will give us 25 files. After you complete this, you are going to have 10 skeleton files, 20 pencil list files, ten city files, and 25 house files. That is 65 files. Sixty-five files will get most students through tests and most business professionals through product knowledge information, training manuals, and other related items. On Day 15, we are actually going to learn how to build as many as 1,000 files. Can you believe that? I personally have about 2900 files. You are going to astound yourself at what your memory is capable of. Now, let's build those files!!

You're going to select five rooms or five sections in your house, and then in each of these five rooms, you're going to have five files. For example, your first room could be a bedroom, and you pick five pieces of furniture. The next room is the kitchen, and you pick five appliances. The next room is the bathroom, and you use five files. Maybe the tub, or toilet or sink. If you live in a small apartment, you still have five sections. A bathroom, a kitchen, a living room, a hall and a bedroom. If you need to use the front yard, parking lot, or driveway, do that. Just choose five sections.

After you have selected the five rooms or sections, then select 5 files in each room. Visualize yourself standing in the doorway of your first room. Then start at the right or the left, it doesn't matter, just so you're consistent. Then going clockwise or counterclockwise, choose five files. Pick big items over small items and spread them out across the room. In other words, don't cram all of your files on one side of the room. Spread them out evenly and avoid using the same items in each room. For example, if you select a chair in one room, don't use a chair in the next. So, in review, select five rooms and five files in each room. If you use your front yard, then make one of the files a pole, another could be the grass, the mailbox and so forth. Right now, make sure you have five rooms (or areas) and five files in each room. Later, if you have more room, feel free to add more files. Right now, keep it at five and five. Don't put six files in one room and four in the next. The reason for that will make sense later.

Here is an example of what one of the rooms might look like.

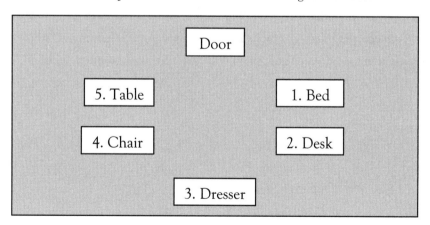

This is where you are going to store information. I just met a lady this week with an ERA real estate office. She took this course a few years ago. She was telling me how much she enjoyed the class and she even took her son to the course. She said that when they moved her son said that they were not done packing. She looked at him like he was crazy. She said, "Of course we are!" He said, "No, Mom. I've still got my pictures hanging all over the files in the kitchen. I can't get them off. Every time I look in there, I see them." Now, that's a good imagination, and the kind we all need to have to make this system work. But don't worry, you can move and even rearrange your furniture because in your mind is where the files exist and they stay the same in there.

I have created these mental journeys in every home I have ever lived in. I have also created journeys through my friend's homes. This will be a great exercise for you too. After you create your own house files I strongly encourage you to create a map like this of your family member's and friend's homes. You could easily create 200-300 files in just a few hours doing this.

Now for the instruction on how to do this: The first room is going to be one through five, the second room is going to be six through ten, the third room is going to be 11 through 15, the fourth room is 16 through 20, and the fifth room is 21 through 25. The best thing that you can do right now is make sure you have these 25 files created and review them until you know them cold without hesitation the number and the file.

day 10

Poems and Quotes

Welcome to Day ten. Did you enjoy building your house files yesterday? I hope so. I can't stress enough how much I like the house files and how often I use them. As a matter of fact, we're going to use our house files right now! We are going to memorize a 20-line poem. That's right. We are going to learn a 20-line poem forwards, backwards and by number. Are you ready? First of all I would like you to read this poem through once or twice just to get a feel for it. Don't try to memorize it just now, simply read it and get a feel for it.

The Man in the Glass
By Dale Wimbrow

When you get what you want in your struggle for self
And the world makes you king for a day.
Just go to a mirror and look at yourself
And see what that man has to say.
For it is not your father, your mother or your wife
Whose judgment upon you must pass.
But the fellow's verdict who counts most in your life is the man
looking back from the glass.
Some people may say you are a square shooting chum
And call you a wonderful guy.
But the man in the glass says you're only a bum,
If you can't look him straight in the eye.
He is the one to please, never mind the rest,

For he's with you clear up until the end.
And you will pass your most dangerous and difficult test
If the man in the glass is your friend.
You may fool the whole world down the pathway of years
And get pats on your back as you pass.
But your final reward will be heartache and tears
If you've cheated the man in the glass.

That is a pretty powerful poem, isn't it? Every time I use it in a seminar, I always get quite a reaction. When memorizing a poem (or quotes, scripture, etc) we never turn every word into a picture. Instead, after reading each line or verse, we create a picture that will be a brain trigger for that line. I'm going to give you 20 pictures that you are going to file to your first 20 files. As we do this, look at each line of the poem that corresponds with the number. If you prefer to use your own pictures, then by all means, do that. Mine are just suggestions, but use what works for you. We are going to use our house files.

1.) File two people who look exactly like you and they are struggling or wrestling with each other.

2.) Sitting on top of a globe with a king's crown on.

3.) You looking in a mirror

4.) A man talking

5.) Your mother, your father and your wife (or spouse or what you would imagine they looked like if you had one!)

6.) Judge in a car and you are passing him

7.) Jury foreman standing up and giving a verdict on your life.

8.) A man in a mirror looking back at you.

9.) Gun that shoots square gum.

10.) File Jimmy Stewart from *It's A Wonderful Life*.

11.) A mirror with a reflection what you consider a bum to be. (For me, it is the 1954 Dodgers. They were referred to them as bums.)

12.) A huge eyeball that you can't stand to look at

13.) Someone begging you please, maybe there's a lot of people behind him and you pay no attention to the rest

14.) A man running a race and he is crossing the finish line

15.) Student passing a test

16.) Your best friend in a glass

17.) An old fool walking down a pathway

18.) Someone patting you on the back as you pass them

19.) Someone handing you a trophy and you start crying and your heart breaks

20.) Stealing from the man in the glass

Now write down these 20 lines. Don't write the story necessarily or the file, just the picture you saw. If you got stuck on one, don't worry about it. Move on to the next. We are not concerned with perfect scores. We are in the learning stage. So, stop now and fill in one through 20. DON'T try and write down the poem word for word just the images that you saw. Later you can make sure the images are brain triggers for you for the poem.

Well, how did you do? Did you get 17 or more? If you did, that is very good. If you got a perfect score, that's even better! Now, remember, when you memorize scripture or lines of a poem, you don't turn every single word into a picture. You simply use brain triggers are going to be cues for you. Remember that your mind works like a computer and the glue must be strong for you. That is what holds the picture or data in place. The glue is the circuit board of your memory. Before we wrap up the lesson for the day, let's go through and review the poem just so you are clear what the pictures represent.

Number one, two people struggling. The line of poetry is, when you get what you want in your struggle for self. Number two, a man sitting on top of a globe wearing a king's crown, and the world makes you king for a day. Number three, looking at your reflection in the mirror, just go to a mirror and look at yourself. Number four, a man talking, and see what that man has to say. Number five, your father, your mother, and your wife, the poetry says, for it is not your father, or your mother or your wife. Number six, a judge passing you in a car. The poem says, whose judgment upon you must pass. Number seven, a jury for man giving a verdict in your life. The poem says, but the fellow's verdict who counts most in your life. Number eight, a man's reflection in the mirror. The poem says, is the man looking back from the glass. Number nine, a gun that shoots square gum, some people may call you a square shooting chum. Number ten, Jimmy Stewart in *It's A Wonderful Life*, and call you a wonderful guy.

Number 11, a mirror and your idea of what a bum looks like. The poetry says, but the man in the glass says you're only a bum. Number 12, a huge eye that you can't look straight at. The poetry says, if you can't look him straight in the eye. Number 13, someone with their hands folded begging you please with the rest of the people behind him. The poetry says, for he is the one to please, never mind the rest. Number 14, a runner crossing a finish line. The poetry says, for he is with you clear up till the end. Number 15, a student passing a test. The poem says, you will pass your most dangerous and difficult test. Number 16, your best friend in a glass. The poetry says, if the man in the glass is your friend. Number 17, an old fool walking down a pathway. The poetry says, you may fool the whole world down the pathway of years. Number 18, someone patting you on the back as you pass. The poem says, and get pats on your back as you pass. Number 19, someone handing you a trophy and it breaks your heart and you start to cry. The poetry says, your final reward will be heartache and tears. And, finally, number 20, someone stealing from the man in the glass. The poem says, if you have cheated the man in the glass. Wow! Do you realize what you just did? You just memorized a twenty line poem forwards, backwards, and by number.

You might have to read the poem once or twice to fill in the blanks if the pictures don't make one hundred per cent sense to you. But give yourself some credit. I know that if you would have seen me looking at a poem for five minutes and then have been able to say the poem forwards, backwards, and by number, you would probably have been incredibly impressed with my memory. So, give yourself the same amount of credit that you would give me. You just accomplished something very remarkable. Soon, you will learn how to give speeches without notes and retain product knowledge. The skill you just learned is tremendous for lines of poetry, scriptures or quotations.

day 11

Memorizing Sales Presentations

Welcome back. It's Day 11. Have you been reciting *The Man in the Glass*? It is a great poem. It is extremely powerful. I conclude our workshop with it and it is a powerful way to end this seminar. It really strikes a chord with some people. If you are a public speaker, this system will allow you to incorporate poems and quotations that draw your audience in. Also, I think it's a good point to remind you not to get caught up in being perfect.

Perhaps you have heard the story of Thomas Edison when he was constructing the light bulb. It took him over 1,000 attempts. After he successfully completed the light bulb, he held a press conference and a brash reporter asked him, "Mr. Edison, how does it make you feel to have failed over 1,000 times?" Mr. Edison without missing a beat, promptly responded, "You misunderstand. I did not fail over 1,000 times. I successfully found 1,000 ways the light bulb will not work." Now, that's a positive attitude. And it is an attitude that we can learn from for sure.

If you don't get a perfect score, do what Mr. Edison did. Ask yourself why. Learn something from the failure. Remember it was for one of two reasons. It was either number one, you didn't know your file, or number two, your circuit board or your action was not strong enough. Those are the only two reasons. So learn a lesson from Mr. Edison. The skill that I want to teach you next is how to give a sales presentation or, for that matter, any presentation without using notes. This is a money making skill.

The file system I use to give my presentation is my skeleton files. What are the skeleton files? Remember, they are top, nose, mouth, ribs, liver, joint, cap, fibula, ball and sand. That is where we are going to store a generic sales presentation. Let's say that you are a new salesperson or a veteran salesperson who would like to nail your presentation down a little better. What do you do? You break it down into separate thoughts, then turn those thoughts into pictures and file them to your files. So, I'm going to give you ten items and you need to scan through these very quickly. These items are going to represent the steps in a sales presentation. Most companies have a presentation that at the end has a call for action, and the presentation is designed in a very specific manner. There, most likely, is psychology behind the presentation, and all too often, a salesperson will get caught up in the moment and forget the steps in his presentation which weaken it. So, your presentation may or may not be similar to the one we're about to learn. However, after you do this exercise, you should have a very good understanding of a very practical business application to this system that we are learning.

File these pictures to your files **as fast as you can**. Make the pictures vivid and **KEEP MOVING!!**

1.) Handshake for the introduction.
2.) Statistics (to back up the value of your product)
3.) Professional giving an opinion
4.) Asking questions
5.) Filling a need (what your product accomplishes)
6.) Demonstration
7.) Features and benefits
8.) Testimonials or third party references
9.) Investment
10.)Call to action

Okay, scan through it one more time if you have to and then stop and write these ten items down.

How did you do? If you got all ten, give yourself a pat on the back for a job well done. If you missed one, be sure to ask yourself why. Did you know your file and was your picture vivid enough? Give yourself some credit if you scored well. Remember, that if you would have given me ten pictures rapidly and then I recited them back forwards, backwards, and by number, you would be very impressed. Well, guess what? That is what you just did. Now, for the practical application, this is what I use when I give my sales presentation. I file it to my skeleton files. If you were just learning a presentation or if you were a veteran, this will help you. You could even help a coworker learn this presentation.

Remember that not everyone has benefited from our training, and when you see a young salesperson struggling to learn the steps of the presentation, tell him to build files in his office and then use pictures as brain triggers. By the way, some of you may say, "Well, Ronnie, what if I file the ten major points of my presentation but there are details under each one that I can't recall? In this situation, what you would do is file the ten major points, then if there is more information that you want to file, file that on top. Go back and *layer* them on. Remember, the Mount Rainier story taught us that we could link items together and file them together. For example, we could file Mount Rainier to the top of your head right now and we would actually have 19 items on that file. So, the principle is the same if you have more than one item to file to each file. Go back and layer them on top of one another. That is what I did for my sales presentation. After I was sure I had the ten major points, I went back and filed minor points on top of the major ones. There you have it a sales presentation without notes!

day 12

Uses For Files

Now, let's learn a little bit about learning product knowledge. If you are a student, this will still apply to you because you can see how this will help you study for a test. I will show you as we go. We are going to use our house files for product knowledge. We have five rooms and five files in each room. In this scenario, we are going to be an automobile salesperson. However, this would work effectively if you sold copiers, homes, mortgages, insurance or something else. As a salesperson, you not only want to know the features and benefits of your product, you also want to know the benefits of similar models competitors may have. This is the way to handle that. You dedicate your first room to the product knowledge about your product.

Pick five key selling features of your product and file them to your files. Remember, we are going to use the example of being an automobile sales professional for this one. So, let's say you are focusing on sports utility vehicles and you are a Toyota salesman. What you do is take the five selling features and file them to your first room. Perhaps it is leg room to one file, financing to another, sunroof to another. Whatever the five key selling features are, file them to your first five files. Now, you ask, "What are the next four rooms for?" Good question. I'm glad that you asked. Each one of these rooms is dedicated to your competition. That's right, you are going to dedicate a room of your house to your competition. So, you make room number two, your Mazda room, room three, your Jeep room, room four, your Chevy room, room five, your Lincoln Mercury room. Then in each one of these rooms, you list the five benefits over theirs. Be creative and use your own imagination. If you're a copy machine sales professional, one room could be your Xerox room, one your Panasonic and so on.

If you so desired, you could fill up all 25 files with information on your product. The reason I throw in competition information is that people are comfortable doing business with the salesperson who knows a lot about the sales industry. That includes how their product measures up to the competition. If you are a student, you can use this same concept in studying for a test. Let's say you are taking a history test and you need to learn to major causes of the Civil War. You make one room your Civil War room, and you file the causes for the Civil War to that room. The next thing you might need to know are the major battles of the Civil War, so you file those in that room. The third room may be some important dates in the Civil War, and so on. This is just an example. However, you use the same concept as product knowledge. You can dedicate each room to a particular theme and then file information to that room. I recall studying for a psychology test one day, and the first room, I filed five major psychologists. The second room I used to file theories. The third room was to experiments, and I continued until I had all my notes on my files. For students, I would also encourage that you file rooms in your class. I remember when I was in school looking out the window and the teacher would say, "Ronnie, the answer isn't on the window." Well, guess what? It might just be in this case. If you are a student or a business professional, room files are a great way to group thoughts or ideas by room. It helps to organize them in your mind.

The activity today is going to be a little different. You know what situation you're in. Perhaps you need to recall product knowledge or perhaps test information is more important to you. Use your house files if you are a salesperson who needs to file product knowledge to your files just like we talked about. It may take a moment to sit down and actually do, however, even if you are a veteran sales professional, I think you will be astounded at the new information that you can store even if it is about your competitors. If you are in the business arena, but not as a salesperson, then file information pertinent to your job. Perhaps it could be procedures or new training you are learning. If you are a student, this should be a "gimme". Get out you notes for your next test and file them to your 25 house files. Remember that you can group them by room. Do it! And do not continue to the next lesson until you have done so. Remember that your final reward will be heartache and tears if you've cheated the man in the glass. So, don't cheat the man in the glass. Fill up your 25 files with something that is going to be a benefit to you and we will talk again tomorrow. Have a great day and get going!

day 13

Giving Speeches Without Notes

Welcome to Day 13. How did your exercises go yesterday? That was your first real test of something that you have to memorize every day. I'm confident that you found the room files very easy to use and extremely helpful. So far, we have filed information to our skeleton files, our house files, city files and the pencil list. That is all the files we are going to create together. So, at this point in the program, you have all the files that you are going to need to get through most everything. On Day 15, I will cover how to build up to 1,000 files. Yes, you heard that right, 1,000. Today, we are going to learn how to give speeches without the use of notes.

According to a survey that came out a few years ago, the number one fear in America is the fear of public speaking. The number two fear on that survey was the fear of death. Can you believe that? People are terrified of giving a speech. However, when you can give a speech without notes, it builds your credibility, your self esteem, you are able to maintain eye contact and the people you are talking to are impressed with your subject matter. They will notice when you aren't using notes. I instruct our live two-day seminars and I never access a single note. That is seven hours each day and 14 hours total, and I never use a single note. Well, actually I'm using notes. I'm just the only one that can see my notes. To instruct our seminars, I take my notes and then file them to my house files. I do not memorize my speech word for word. Imagine how boring that would be to listen to a speech that had been memorized word for word. Instead, I just file the major thoughts to my files and then jump from one file to the next in my mind. If you are called upon to give a speech, it will be most likely on a subject that you're familiar with. So you will not need to recall it word for word. Instead, you will use brain triggers to move from one file to the next. Let me show you what I mean.

I'm going to give you ten pictures and then file these pictures to your house files. You are only going to use your first two rooms because I am going to give you ten pictures. These ten pictures are actually ten items from a speech given on time management. Remember, we are going to use our house files. So sit back, relax, close your eyes, and think house files.

Here are the items. Memorize these as rapidly as you can! Try to just go through each word once and only a few seconds per word.

1.) Clock
2.) Organizer or day planner
3.) "things to do" list
4.) Goal post to number 4
5.) Cargo ship importing ants
6.) Black jack dealer standing behind a gate
7.) Fun
8.) Calendar
9.) Work room
10.) Blueprints with glue

You know the drill, write these down and see how many that you get. Remember that you only need to write the picture down. Not the action or the files.

How did you do? Did you get all of them? If you didn't, it's for only one of two reasons. Either number one, you didn't know your file or number two, your picture wasn't vivid enough. There is no other possible reason. When you give a speech without notes, you never memorize it word for word. Instead you have brain triggers to keep you moving from one thought to the next. So, what we have here is ten brain triggers that will get us talking about ten major points. Follow along as I show you what I mean. This is a speech on time management.

The first thing that you open your speech with is time management. That is why we filed the clock to the number one file. Remember that the code our mind uses to recall information is pictures, so we used a clock to represent time management. You used this brain trigger to introduce the subject of your speech to your audience.

The next thing that you talk about was filed to your number two file. What did we file to your number two file? It was an organizer. The word we want to talk about is being organized. After you see this prompt on your file, you can go into more depth with your audience and perhaps talk with them about using a day timer or a Franklin planner or getting organized using a program where there are computers or simply a filing system at their office.

Number three, what is your file? What did you file to it? A "things to do list", right? Talk to your group about the importance of writing out a "things to do list" every day. That way, you have a plan for the day and they day does not simply happen around you.

Number four, what is your file? What did you file to it? A goal post, right? This represents that you must set and establish goals to be organized. At this point you may mention the importance of setting goals with a deadline and clearly define objectives.

Now, number five. What did we file to number five? Ants. Being imported, right? This represents the word importance. You are importing ants. This is a mental cue to remind you that you need to select an importance on each item on your things to do list and make certain items a priority. Notice we are not memorizing every single word. Just key words that are going to become brain triggers.

Number six, what did we file to number six? A black jack dealer behind a gate. The word we wanted to recall is delegate. We used a dealer for del and gate for gate. So, we have delegate for number six. This is important to mention when you are assigning tasks for individuals and not trying to tackle the project on your own.

Number seven, what is your file? What did we file to it? We filed fun to that file. When you see this, remind your audience that it's important to set time aside for fun. All work and no play is not good. You must allocate time to let your mind relax and have some fun.

Number eight, what is your file? What did we file to it? You filed a schedule. When you see the schedule, you'll remember that this is a brain trigger to talk about keeping a regular schedule and getting up the same time every day and make a routine. This will help you to use your time more wisely.

Number nine, you are going to talk about setting up a special room to work in. This is a place where you can go and get away from all distractions and just focus on work.

Number ten, we filed a blueprint with glue on it. That means that as you review your speech and recap the highlights, reinforce your audience the importance of having a plan and sticking to it. That is what the glue symbolizes. Sticking to it.

Now, you understand the concept of how to give a speech without notes. It is not important to memorize every word. Just make brain triggers and then file them to your files. Giving speeches without notes is an exclusive skill, and one that will increase your confidence when you master it. I encourage you to concentrate on this skill. It is a powerful one.

day 14

Foreign Languages

Welcome back. It's Day 14. How did you like learning how to give speeches without notes yesterday? That is a useful skill for business professionals as well as students who are called on to give speeches in their class. I encourage you to go back and use this skill if you have to.

A lot of people want to learn foreign languages but don't know where to start. They will get on the treadmill and put on the foreign language tapes. Now this is better than nothing, but let's remind ourselves that our minds work like a computer and we can use this to our benefit when we want to recall something. On Day seven, we learned how to count in Japanese. We did this by turning the first ten numbers of Japanese into English pictures and then filed them to our pencil list. You could have just as easily turned French numbers, German, Hebrew or even Latin into pictures and then file them to your files. Counting in a foreign language is not that hard at all when you approach it from the correct angle. And that angle would be to use our system. Focus, location, code, action and review

Here are some words that you don't see often:

Sire	Jontar
Nosh	Pie
Morangu	Puegas
Pesagu	Payne
Bosa	Pastage

These are ten words that are definitely not English. However, using the concept that our minds use the code of pictures to recall, we can very easily file these away. We are not going to actually stick these pictures on any of our organized file lists. Instead, we are going to file these pictures to their definitions. Follow along and you'll see what I mean.

The first word is sire. This is the Portuguese word for a woman's skirt. Visualize a woman's skirt sighing. It is a sire (sigh-er). You'll never forget that. The word is sire and the definition is a woman's skirt.

The next word is the Portuguese word, nosh, meaning walnut. Visualize yourself eating a giant walnut and it makes you nauseous. The word is nosh and it means walnut.

The next word is morangu and it means strawberry in Portuguese. See a gigantic strawberry eating a meringue pie. The word is morangu and the definition is strawberry.

The next word is pesagu. This is Portuguese for peach. See a giant peach asking you to pass the goo. That's right. A giant peach asking you to, 'Pass the goo.' The word is pesagu and the definition is peach.

The next word is bosa, and it's Portuguese for a woman's purse. See a large piece of balsa wood carrying a woman's purse. You look out your window and you see a large piece of balsa wood carrying a woman's purse, that would be a picture that sticks in your mind. The word is bosa and the Portuguese definition is purse.

The next word is jontar and it is Portuguese for dinner. Now, file a man named John and he is eating tar for dinner. A man named John and he is eating tar for dinner. The word is jontar and the definition is dinner.

The next word is pie and it is Portuguese for father. See yourself throwing a pie in your father's face. Hit your father in the face with a pie. The word is pie and the definition is father.

The next word is puegas and it is Portuguese for socks. Visualize some socks that have a really bad odor and you say, "Piew, that smells like gas!" The word puegas and the definition is gas.

The next word is pan, and it is French for bread. See a pan and the handle is made of bread. The word is pan and the definition is bread. The final word is pastake. Pastake, and it is French for watermelon. See a watermelon passing a deck of cards to you. The word is pastake and the definition is watermelon.

Now, as you can see, learning a foreign language is very simple. You must turn it into a picture and then file it to its definition. Any word can be turned into a picture or something can be substituted for it. You have just learned a little bit of French and Portuguese! Can you believe that? It was pretty painless, wasn't it?

Let's see how many definitions that you can recall now. Fill in the blanks below with the defintitions:

1.) Saia_____

2.) Noz_____

3.) Morangoo_____

4.) Passego_____

5.) Bolsa_____

6.) Jantar_____

7.) Pai_____

8.) Peugas_____

9.) Pain_____

10.) Pasteque_____

So, how did you do? Did you get all of them? If you didn't, ask yourself why. Was your picture vivid enough? The code your mind thinks in is pictures and you must make the pictures very strong. Now, I want you to understand that this concept we just learned for foreign language can also be used for English words. Have you ever learned words that are new to you? Sure you have. Even in English, I would dare say there are many words that in some fashion or form are foreign to you. Use the same concept that we used for foreign languages. For example, take the word neophyte. It's an English word. It means beginner. What if you saw a boxing match or a fight and the boxers were on their knees. They would be a knee fight, wouldn't it? So, we turn the word into a picture and the word is beginner. So, we have the audience as a bunch of bees and they're drinking gin. It's a knee fight with bees drinking gin. That is a picture that you wouldn't forget even if you tried. Make it a goal of yours to learn a foreign language or expand upon the one you already know. Purchase an audio program or a book and learn a few words a day or a week with this method. At the end of the year, I think you'll be impressed with your vocabulary. And remember this quote that I live by, "A year from now you will have wished you started today." So, seize the day with your new found skills.

day 15

Intro to Number Memory

Welcome back. It's Day 15. Are you bilingual yet? Well, you'll get there if it is a goal of yours and put this system into practice. You will amaze yourself if you do everything your mind is capable of doing. What we are about to learn is a very useful skill. I find that it is so useful that I'm going to spend three days on it. I hope you are ready to really expand your memory capabilities. This is going to be a skill that if you master it, you will astound people with your memory.

I'm going to show you how to memorize a 100 digit number after just hearing it once! March 7th, 2009 I actually memorized a 167 digit number in five minutes to set a new USA record. When my friends get bored, they will write out a series of numbers and I will do this demonstration. It never fails to get quite a reaction. However, it is very simple and it is also very useful. I use this skill to memorize phone numbers. When I was a student, I used to recall dates and other important numbers. This is somewhat an advanced skill, so don't worry if it doesn't make 100% sense the first time. This is something that you may have to review three or four times to understand the concept.

What are the five things that you need to memorize something or anything? They are focus, location, code, action and review. When recalling a number, the location is no problem. We could use our house files, skeleton files, city files or even the pencil list. The challenge is the code or the pictures. Numbers are abstract and must be turned into a picture before we can recall them. We turned one through 20 into pictures using basic association on the pencil list. However, it is sometimes hard to think of an association for every number. For example, what is an association for 86? That would be a challenge and most likely require some thought. What if I told you that there's a system to turning numbers into pictures. That's right! There is a system. This is not a new system at all. It has been around for quite some time.

This system was actually introduced more than 300 years ago by Stonsen Mink Vonwesenhein. Vonwesenhein's basic construction was modified by Dr. Richard Gray, an Englishman. The major system was devised to allow the master memorizers of the time to break the bonds of the previously excellent but more limited systems. This system was developed to memorize long digit numbers.

For every number from zero to nine, a consonant sound is assigned to that letter. The sounds have been assigned to these numbers for hundreds of years since Dr. Richard Gray. Here they are:

0 = Suh

1 = Tuh

2 = Nuh

3 = Muh

4 = Ruh

5 = Luh

6 = Juh

7 = Kuh

8 = Fuh

9 = Buh

All you have to do is memorize these. Does that sound like a challenge?

What if I told you that I bet you could learn these in less than a minute? What if I told you already memorized them. That's right, you've already memorized these. I already taught them to you. Remember when I told you that everything in this course is done for a reason and I'm actually going to teach you things that you are not even using yet? Well, here's an example of that. Remember when we learned our skeleton files? Let's review what our files were. Top, nose, mouth, ribs, liver, joint, cap, fibula, ball and sand. Now, let's review the phonic sounds. They are tuh, nuh, muh, ruh, luh, shuh, juh, cuh, fuh, puh or buh and suh. Did you catch that? Let's go slow this time. The consonant sound assigned to number one is tuh, and the first skeleton file is top. So number one is t that has the tuh sound. The letter assigned to number two is n because it has the nuh sound and the second skeleton file is nose. So number two is n for nuh. The letter assigned to the number three is m and our third skeleton file is mouth. Number three is m. The letter assigned to four is ruh. The fourth skeleton file is ribs. Number four is ruh, or r. Four is repre-sented by r or ruh. The fifth skeleton file is liver, and the letter as-signed to number five is l. Five is l or luh. That is easy enough, isn't it?

However, once you get this down, it's going to catapult your memory to the expert memory level. The letter assigned to six is juh or shuh and the sixth skeleton file is joint. Joint represents the j or juh. The letter assigned to your seventh file is a hard c sound or k. Kuh. And the seventh skeleton file is cap. Seven is a hard c or a k. The letter assigned to the number eight is f or v. Your eighth skeleton file is f or v. Your eighth skeleton file is your fibula. Number eight is f or v, or fuh or vuh. The letter assigned to your number nine is puh or buh, p and b. And your ninth skeleton file is ball. So, number nine is p or b. And finally, the last skeleton file is actually number ten, but for the purposes of this system, this will represent the number zero. Zero is assigned to a soft c or s. Zero is the suh sound.

The ten primary phonetic sounds are tuh, nuh, muh, ruh, luh, shuh, juh, kuh, fuh, puh or buh and suh. Stop now and review your skeleton files and make sure that you know the sounds one through ten where ten is actually representing zero. Make sure that you know them.

Here are a few examples of how you would use this system to turn numbers into pictures. Remember we only add vowels.

Number	Phonetic Sound	Picture
35	3 = M 5 = L	MaLL
72	7 = C 2 = N	CaN
59	5 = L 9 = P	LaP
25	2 = N 5 = L	NaiL

Now you try:

Number	Phonetic Sound	Picture
17	1 = ___ 7 = ___	_____
47	4 = ___ 7 = ___	_____
79	7 = ___ 9 = ___	_____
24	2 = ___ 4 = ___	_____
14	1 = ___ 4 = ___	_____
83	8 = ___ 3 = ___	_____
56	5 = ___ 6 = ___	_____
38	3 = ___ 8 = ___	_____
49	4 = ___ 9 = ___	_____
95	9 = ___ 5 = ___	_____
82	8 = ___ 2 = ___	_____
55	5 = ___ 5 = ___	_____
45	4 = ___ 5 = ___	_____
77	7 = ___ 7 = ___	_____
29	2 = ___ 9 = ___	_____

So, how did you do? Does this take some getting used to? You better believe it! Have you ever turned numbers into pictures this way before? I bet not. So, if it seems a little bit unusual to you, don't worry about it! However, you most likely never have attempted before to memorize a 100-digit number. To do something you have never done before, you must learn things that you have never learned before.

Here are my pictures for numbers 1-100.

1 – Hat	26 – Notch	51 – Light	76 – Cash
2 – Hen	27 – Neck	52 – Lane	77 – Kicking
3 – Ham	28 – Knife	53 – Lame	78 – Cough
4 – Hair	29 – Nap	54 – Lure	79 – Cap
5 – Hail	30 – Mice	55 – Lily	80 – Face
6 – Hash	31 – Mat	56 – Leash	81 – Fat
7 – Hook	32 – Moon	57 – Lock	82 – Fan
8 – Ivy	33 – Mom	58 – Leaf	83 – Foam
9 – Hoop	34 – Mare	59 – Lap	84 – Fire
10 – Ties	35 – Mall	60 – Juice	85 – File
11 – Dot	36 – Match	61 – Jet	86 – Fish
12 – Tin (can)	37 – Mug	62 – Shin	87 – Fog
13 – Dime	38 – Muff	63 – Gym	88 – Fife (Barney)
14 – Tire	39 – Mop	64 – Jar	89 – Fob
15 – Tile	40 – Rice	65 – Jail	90 – Bus
16 – Dish	41 – Rat	66 – Judge	91 – Pot
17 – Tack	42 – Rain	67 – Shack	92 – Pan
18 – Dove	43 – Ram	68 – Chef	93 – Bum
19 – Top	44 – Rear	69 – Ship	94 – Pour
20 – Nose	45 – Roll	70 – Case	95 – Pool
21 – Net	46 – Rash	71 – Cat	96 – Bush
22 – Nun	47 – Rock	72 – Can	97 – Pack
23 – Name	48 – Roof	73 – Comb	98 – Puff
24 – Nero	49 – Rope	74 – Car	99 – Pipe
25 – Nail	50 – Lice	75 – Coal	100 – Doses

One through nine I use the letter 'H' because it is a silent consonant sound and it helps if you have more than one consonant when creating a word so the letter 'H' helps us out here. Also it is important to note that the following phonetic sounds share a number:

1 = tuh or duh	8 = fuh or vuh
6 = shuh or juh	9 = puh or buh
7 = kuh or guh	

If you move your mouth to make the sounds puh and buh you will see that your mouth moves in the same way. These are phonetically the same. The same is true with the other sounds listed above. This give you more options when creating pictures for numbers.

There is also another method for creating pictures for numbers and this method is referred to as 'Character/Action'. The idea or concept behind this method is that you use a person or character for each number. My character for 88 is Michael Irvin the former wide receiver for the Dallas Cowboys because 88 was his number. The action for 88 for me is receiving a pass.

The challenge with this is that simply looking at each number it can be difficult to think of a person or character that this number reminds you of. That is where the method above for having letters for numbers actually helps. Let's take 77. That is Kuh Kuh. So my character for 77 is 'King Kong' and the action is climbing a building.

Let's do one more, the number 24 is Nuh and Ruh. So my person for 24 is Norris (Chuck) and the action is a karate kick. You can create your own rules here for this method. You can use the letters 'N' and 'R' as initials or sounds of the last name. It is your system so make your own rules!

With this character/action method you can actually recall four digits at a time. Let's take the number 7724. For the first pair of digits use the character and for the second pair of digits you use the action. So 77 would be King Kong and 24 would be a karate kick. You have King Kong delivering a karate kick!

The number 2488 would be Chuck Norris for 24 and receiving a pass for 88. The first set of numbers is the person and the second the action. If you wanted to take it one step further you could develop an object to go with the character/action. The object for 24 could be a board (karate kicking a board), the object for 88 could be a football (catching a football). If you did this you could memorize six digits at a time! This is the method I used when I set the USA record for most numbers memorized in five minutes (167 consecutive digits)

Make sure that you understand Day 15 100% before moving on to Day 16.

day 16

How to Memorize Numbers

We are going to go a little more in depth with phonics today. The best way to practice phonics is every time you hear a number, turn it into a picture. You are going to encounter numbers tomorrow anyway, so you might as well turn them into a picture. When you are driving today, you are going to see an exit sign that will say Exit 56. Turn that into a picture. Say to yourself, five is luh, and six is shuh, so luh and shuh, it's a leash! Whammo, you have just turned 56 into a picture! You may say, "Ronnie, that's a lot of work, and I'm going to have to do that every time I want to remember a number?" Absolutely not. You are going to have to do that the first time only. The next time you run across 56, you've already turned it into a picture.

Initially, you are going to have to go through the steps when you want to turn 56 into a picture. However, the next time the work is already done. When I hear numbers today, I am no longer turning them into a picture. I already have the pictures.

I'm going to give you 35 pictures and you are going to file them to your house files for 1-25 and your skeleton files for 26-35. Each one of these pictures is representative of a number.

I am going to encourage you to set a timer for 5 minutes for this next exercise. If you finish before the five minutes is up GREAT, if not do your best to finish in five minutes. You will have memorized a 70 digit number in five minutes if you do this. Currently the United States record is 160 digits in five minutes and 70 digits is VERY respectable. Don't beat yourself up if you don't get them all but let's shoot for it.

Here are the words. Place 1-25 on your house files and 26-35 on your skeleton files.

1.) Nail	19.) Tire
2.) Can	20.) Fish
3.) Juice	21.) Jet
4.) Moon	22.) Rat
5.) Mall	23.) Mom
6.) Match	24.) Foam
7.) Bus	25.) Case
8.) Tin	26.) Rat
9.) Fire	27.) Pan
10.) Chef	28.) Pack
11.) Mop	29.) Nap
12.) Pool	30.) Leash
13.) Ship	31.) Mall
14.) Dove	32.) Jar
15.) Cat	33.) File
16.) Pipe	34.) Leaf
17.) Dish	35.) Shack
18.) Shin	

Now, stop and write these words out 1-35.

You just memorized a 70 digit number! Here it is:

1.) Nail = 25	19.) Tire = 14
2.) Can = 72	20.) Fish = 86
3.) Juice = 60	21.) Jet = 61
4.) Moon = 32	22.) Rat = 41
5.) Mall =35	23.) Mom = 33
6.) Match =36	24.) Foam = 83
7.) Bus = 90	25.) Case = 70
8.) Tin = 12	26.) Rat = 41
9.) Fire = 84	27.) Pan = 92
10.) Chef = 68	28.) Pack = 97
11.) Mop = 39	29.) Nap = 29
12.) Pool = 95	30.) Leash = 56
13.) Ship = 69	31.) Mall = 35
14.) Dove = 18	32.) Jar = 64
15.) Cat = 71	33.) File = 85
16.) Pipe = 99	34.) Leaf = 58
17.) Dish = 16	35.) Shack = 67
18.) Shin = 62	

How did you do? Perfect score? Did you get close? This is fun, isn't it?

One important note is for numbers starting with zero. We don't have images for 09, 08, 07, etc. Remember zero is the 'suh' sound. So for 07 it is suh and kuh. My picture for 07 is sack. Go ahead and create your own images for the digits starting with zero and enjoy!

day 17

Pictures for Numbers to 1000

Turning numbers into pictures has many practical applications. It is great for remembering phone numbers, product knowledge, technical data, product codes and more. Personally I have used this method to turn every number between one and 1000 into a picture. The sounds for 127 are 'tuh', 'nuh' and 'kuh'. Therefore my picture for 127 is a tank. Here are my pictures for every number up to 1000!

101 - Toast	116 - Hot dish	133 - Teammate	150 - Tails
102 - Dozen	117 - Tie tack	134 - Timer	151 - Toilet
103 - Decimal	118 - Tooth filling	135 - Oatmeal	152 - Talon
104 - Dessert	119 - Tadpole	136 - Time sheet	153 - Toll man
105 - Diesel	120 - Tennis	137 - Tomahawk	154 - Tailor
106 - Dosage	121 - Tent	138 - Steam fitter	155 - Taillight,
107 - Desk	122 - Tenant	139 - Dimple	156 - Tool shed
108 - Adhesive	123 - Dynamite	140 - Trees,	157 - Telegram
(tape)	124 - Diner	141 - Turtle	158 - Telephone
109 - Teaspoon	125 - Tunnel	142 - Train	159 - Tulip
110 - Tights	126 - Dungeon	143 - Trampoline	160 - Dishes
111 - Dotted	127 - Tank	144 - Dryer	161 - Touchdown
112 - Titanic	128 - Tinfoil	145 - Drill	162 - Station
113 - Totem	129 - Tin pan	146 - Trash	163 – Taj Mahal
(pole)	130 - Damsel,	147 - Truck	164 - T-shirt
114 - Theater	131 - Tomato	148 - Trophy	165 - Dash light
115 - State line	132 - Diamond	149 - Tripod	166 - Head judge

167 - Stagecoach

168 - Dish full

169 - Tissue paper

170 - Taxi

171 - Ticket

172 - Token

173 - Document

174 - Tiger

175 - Tackle

176 - Dictionary

177 - Digging

178 - Takeoff

(airplane)

179 - Teacup

180 - Thieves

181 - Divot

182 - Typhoon

183 - TV man

184 - Diver

185 – Devil

186 - Hot fudge

187 - Stuffing

188 - Dive off

189 - Stove pipe

190 - Tubes, tubs

191 - Teapot

192 - Headband

193 - Topmast

194 - Typewriter

195 - Table

196 - Top shelf

197 – Top Coat

198 - Deep Freeze

199 - Hot pepper

200 - Noses

201 - Nest

202 - Ensign

203 - Newsman

204 - Newsreel

205 - Nozzle

206 - Incision

207 - Unicycle

208 - News ven-dor

209 - Newspaper

210 - Nudist

211 - Handout

212 - Antenna

213 - Ointment

214 - Internet

215 - Noodle

216 - Nutshell

217 - Nightgown

218 - Native

219 - Notebook

220 - Onions

221 - Noontime (face of Clock)

222 - Neon nest

223 - Onion meal

224 - Onion ring

225 - Union hall

226 - Union Jack (Flag)

227 - Nanny goat

228 - Neon foot

229 - Neon pins

230 - Gnomes

231 - Inmate

232 - Honeymoon (Niagara Fall)

233 - New member (club)

234 - Numeral

235 – Animal

236 - Animation (cartoon)

237 - New microphone

238 - Nymph

239 – Nameplate

240 - Nurse

241 - Narrator

242 - No running (sign)

243 - Unarmed

244 - Honorary (degree)

245 - one-reel

246 - Nourishment (food)

247 - New York

248 - Nerve

249 - Unwrap (sandwich)

250 – Nails

251 - Unload

252 – Nylon

253 - Newly made

(Fresh Bread)

254 - Inhaler

255 - Nail hole

256 - Unleash (dog)

257 - Nail cup

258 - Nail file

259 - Nail polish

260 - Notches

261 - Unshod

262 - Engine

263 - in gym

264 - Insurance (policy)

265 - Enchilada

266 - Hinge joint

267 - Inject (needle)

268 - Unshaven

269 – Hunchback

270 - Yankees

271 - Nugget

272 - Noggin (head)

273 – Honeycomb

274 - Anchor

275 - Nickel

276 - Engagement (ring)

277 - Necking

278 - New calf

279 - Innkeeper

280 - Knives

281 - Nevada (Las Vegas)

282 - Infantry

283 - Navy man

284 - University

285 - Navel

286 - Navy ship

287 - Navigator

288 - Knife fight

289 - Navy Pier

290 - Knobs

291 - Neptune

292 - Knee band

293 - Napalm (bomb)

294 - Neighbor

295 - Napoleon

296 - Nuptials (marriage Ceremony)

297 - Napkin

298 - Unpaved

299 - Nabob

300 - Moses

301 - Moustache

302 - Messenger

303 - Museum

304 - Masseur

305 - Missile

306 - Massage

307 - Musket

308 - Mice food

309 - Misprint

310 - Maids

311 - Matador

312 - Mitten

313 - Madam

314 - Mtere

315 - Motel

316 - Midshipman (at Annapolis)

317 - Medical (student)

318 - Mid-field (50-yard line)

319 - Meatball

320 - Mayonnaise

321 - Mint

322 - Manhunt

323 - Monument

324 - Miner

325 - Moonlight

326 - Manager

327 - Mannequin

328 - Manifold (engine)

329 - Money bags

330 - Mummies

331 - Mammoth

332 - Memento

333 - Mamma Mia

334 - Mom reads

335 - Mammal

336 - Mom shouts

337 – M&M Candy

338 - Home movie

339 - Mumps

340 - Mare saddled

341 - Martini

342 - Marine

343 - Mermaid

344 - Mirror

345 - Mural

346 - Martian

347 - Marker

348 - Moor fight

349 - Marble

350 - Mills (fabric mills)

351 - Mullet

352 - Melon

353 - Mailman

354 - Molar (tooth)

355 – Molehill

356 - Mulch

357 - Milk

358 - Mile face

359 - Mailbag, mailbox

360 - Matches

361 - Machete

362 - Mission

363 - Matchmaker

364 - Mushroom

365 - Match holder

366 - Magician

367 - Mashing

368 - Home chef

369 - Matchbook

370 - Hammocks

371 - Macadamia (nut)

372 - Mechanic

373 - Homecoming

374 - Microscope

375 - Mogul (skiing)

376 - Mug shot

377 - Home cooking

378 - Megaphone

379 - Makeup

380 - Movies

381 - Amphitheater

382 - Muffin

383 - Movie maker

384 - Mover

385 - Mayflower (pilgrims), Muffler

386 - Movie show

387 - Movie camera

388 - Mafia family

389 - Movie pilot

390 - Embassy

391 - Amputee

392 - Embankment
393 - Map maker
394 - Umpire
395 - Maple (syrup),
396 - Ambush
397 - Hymnbook
398 - Mop face
399 - Humpback (whale)
400 - Roses
401 - Roast
402 - Raisin
403 - Horseman
404 - Razor
405 - Wrestle
406 - Horseshoe
407 - Race course
408 - Receiver
409 - Raspberry
410 - Roadster
411 - Redhead
412 - Red nose
413 - Radioman
414 - Radar
415 - Radial
416 - Radish
417 - Red coat
418 - Artifact (fossil)
419 - Redbreast (Robin)
420 - Rhinoceros

421 - Hornet
422 - Reunion (class)
423 – Rain Main (movie)
424 - Runner
425 - Rain, hail
426 - Ranch
427 - Rank
428 - Rainforest
429 - Rainbow
430 - Arms
431 - Hermit
432 - Roman
433 - Roommate
434 - Armory
435 - Airmail
436 - Armchair
437 - Arm guard
438 - Earmuff
439 - Ramp
440 - Errors (baseball),
441 - Reward (sign)
442 - Warranty
443 - Re-warm
444 - Rear horse (race)
445 - Rear alley
446 - Worship (church)
447 - Rear-guard
448 - Rear view

(mirror)
449 - Hair rope
450 - Rails
451 - Roulette
452 - Airline
453 - Heirloom
454 - Roller
455 – Whale Oil
456 - Relish
457 - Relic
458 - Airlift
459 – Earlobe
460 - Ridges
461 - Ratchet
462 - Russian
463 - Rushmore (Mount)
464 - Rush hour
465 - Ritual
466 - Rush job
467 - Reject
468 - Hair shave
469 - Airship
470 - Rugs
471 - Rocket
472 – Reagan (Ronald)
473 - Rug man
474 - Rocker
475 - Regular
476 - Air gauge
477 - Rock cliff
478 - Rock fall
479 - Rugby

480 - Harvest
481 - Raft
482 - Orphan
483 - Roof man
484 - Roofer
485 - Rifle
486 - Refugee
487 – Ref Call
488 - Revival
489 – Wave Pool
490 - Ribs
491 - Robot
492 - Ribbon
493 - Air bomb
494 - Robber
495 - Ripple
496 - Rubbish
497 – Reebok (Shoe)
498 - Repave
499 - Rope Bull
500 - Lazy Susan
501 - Holster
502 - Lozenge
503 - Wholesome
504 - Lizard
505 - Lysol
506 - Yellow sachet
507 - Alaska (baked)
508 - Lucifer (devil)
509 - Lace pajamas

510 - Lighthouse
511 - Low tide
512 - Lightning
513 - Altimeter
514 - Ladder
515 - Ladle
516 - Late show
517 - Lithograph
518 - lead-off
(baseball)
519 - Ladybug
520 - Aliens
521 - Island
522 - Linen
523 - Lineman
524 - Liner
(baseball),
525 - Linoleum
526 - Lingerie
527 – Lincoln
(Abe)
528 - Lion family
529 – Line-up
530 - Limousine
531 - Helmet
532 - Lemon
533 - Alma mater
534 - Hallmark
535 - Oil hill
536 - Limejuice
537 - Lamb kills
538 - Lamb face
539 - Lamp
540 - Lawyers

541 - Lard
542 - Lure net
543 - Alarm
544 - Lure watch
545 - Laurel
(wreath)
546 - Allergy
(sneezing)
547 - Lark (bird)
548 - Larva
549 - Lure bag
550 - Lilies
551 – Hall Light
552 - Lowland
553 - Oil lamp
554 - Lily wed-
ding
555 - Low lily
556 - Low latch
557 - Lilac
558 - Yellow liver
559 - Lollipop
560 - Latches,
lodges
561 - Lodged
562 - Lotion
563 - Hall chime
564 - Ledger
565 - Oil shale
566 - Ill judge
567 - Latchkey
568 - Low shaft
569 - Oil ship
570 - Legs

571 - Locket
572 - Lagoon
573 - Locomotive
574 - Locker
575 - Legal
576 - Luggage
577 - Leggings
578 - Lake front,
alcove
579 - Helicopter
580 - Leaves,
loaves, olives
581 - Lift
582 - Elephant
583 - Leaf man
584 - Lever
585 - Level
586 – Live Show
587 - Lifeguard
588 - Laughing
589 - Lifeboat
590 - Lips
591 - Halibut
592 - Albino
593 - Album
594 - Librarian
595 - Label
596 – Hill Bush
597 - Law book
598 - Leapfrog
599 - Oil pipe
600 - Cheeses
601 - Chest
602 - Chasing

603 - Chessman
604 - Juicer
605 - Chisel
606 - Cheese shop
607 - Cheesecake
608 - Juice vat
609 - Cheese-
burger
610 - Shades
611 - Shaded
612 - Shut-in
613 - Showtime
614 - Ashtray
615 - Shuttle
616 - Judiciary
(Supreme
Court)
617 - Shotgun
618 - Shut off
(water)
619 - Shot put
620 - Oceans
621 - Giant
622 - Chain noose
623 - Chain male
624 - Shiner
625 - Channel
626 - Chinchilla
627 - Junk
628 - Ocean front
629 - Chin up,
shin bone
630 - Gems
631 - Gummed

632 - Chimney
633 - Jam maker
634 - Shamrock
635 - Gemologist
636 - Gym shoe
637 - Shoemaker
638 - Jam full
639 - Chimp
640 - Cherries
641 - Chariot
642 - Journal
643 - German
644 - Juror
645 - Cheerleader
646 - Charge
647 - Shark
648 - Giraffe
649 - Cherry pie
650 - Jailhouse
651 - Gelatin
652 - Chow line
653 - Jail man
654 - Jewelry
655 - Shell hole
656 - Jail shade
657 - Chalk
658 - Jellyfish
659 - Jailbird
660 - Judges
661 - judged
(condemned
Man)
662 - Shoe shine
663 - Judgment

(day)
664 - Cheshire cat
665 - Judge law-
yers
666 - Judge show-
down
667 - Judge kids
668 - Shoe shuf-
fling
669 - Shoe shop
670 - Cheeks
671 - Jacket
672 - Chicken
673 - Jackhammer
674 - Joker
675 - Chocolate
676 - Ejection
677 - Jockey kick
678 - chock-full
(of nuts)
679 - Checkbook
680 - Chefs
681 - Shaft
682 - Chiffon
683 - chief-mate
(Navy)
684 - Chauffeur
685 - Javelin
686 - Chef show
687 - Chef cake
688 - Shave off (a
beard)
689 - Chef bakes
690 - Chaps

691 - Chapter
(book)
692 - Jawbone
693 - Chipmunk
694 - Shipwreck
695 - Shoplifter
696 - Egyptian
697 - Shopkeeper
698 – Shop Lifter
699 - Ship builder
700 - Kisses
701 - Cassette
702 - Cousin
703 - Casement
704 - Geyser
705 - Gasoline
706 - Quiz show
707 - Casket
708 - Goose foot
709 - Gazebo
710 - Kites
711 - Cathedral
712 - Cotton
713 - Catamaran
714 - Guitar
715 - Cattle
716 - Cottage
717 - Catacomb
718 - Catfish
719 - Octopus
720 - Gunnysack
721 - Candle
722 - Cannon
723 - Gunman

724 - Canary
725 - Kennel
726 - Gunshot
(wound)
727 - Eggnog
728 - Convict
729 - Canopy
730 - Chemist
731 - Comet
732 – Com-
mander
733 - Comb, men
734 - Camera
735 - Camel
736 - Gumshoe
737 - Kamikaze
738 - Camouflage
739 - Camp
740 - Corsage
741 - Cardinal
742 - Carnation
743 - Aquarium
744 - Courier
745 - Corral
746 - Crutch
747 - Cork
748 – Graffiti
749 - Crab
750 - Gallows
751 - Kilt
752 - Gallon
753 - Column
754 - Caller
755 - Galley

756 - College
757 - Calk
758 - Cauliflower
759 - Caliper
760 - Coaches
761 - Caged
762 - Cushion
763 - Cashmere
764 - Catcher
765 - Eggshell
766 - Cash, shoe
767 – Cash Cow
768 - Cash fire
769 - Ketchup
770 - Quicksand
771 - Cactus
772 - Coconut
773 - Cucumber
774 - Cockroach
775 - Google
776 - Cowcatcher
777 - Cake, cover
778 – Kickoff (Football)
779 - Cookbook
780 - Caves
781 - Cavity
782 - Coffin
783 - Cave man
784 - Gopher
785 - Gavel
786 - Coffee shop
787 - Coffee cup
788 - Coffee field

789 - Coffee pot
790 - Cowboys
791 - Cupid
792 - Cabin
793 - Cab man
794 - Copper
795 - Cable
796 – Cabbage
797 - Cupcake, hockey puck
798 - Cupful
799 - Copyboy, kabob (shish)
800 - Faces, fuses, vases
801 - Faucet
802 - Pheasant
803 – Face Make up
804 - Officer
805 - Vaseline
806 - Physician
807 - Physique (body builder)
808 - Face-off (hockey)
809 - Vice President, Office boy
810 - Fights, footstool, vats
811 - Faded (blue jeans)
812 - Footnote, evidence (Trial)

813 - Fat man, vitamin
814 - Father, feather, Veterinarian
815 - Fiddle, footlocker
816 - Food show
817 - Vodka, photograph
818 - Photo finish
819 - Football, footpath, Footprint
820 - Fence, fins, vines
821 - Fountain
822 – Phone Nokia
823 - Venom
824 - Vineyard
825 - Funnel
826 - Finish (line)
827 - Vinegar
828 - Fanfare
829 – Fan Belt
830 - Foams
831 - Foam hat
832 - Half-moon
833 - Foam mouth
834 - Femur

835 - Family
836 - Famished
837 - Fumigate
838 – Family Fun
839 - Fumble
840 - Firehouse
841 - Fruit
842 - France
843 - Fireman
844 - Forearm
845 - Overalls
846 – Fresh
847 - Frog
848 - Forefinger
849 - Fireplace
850 - Fleece (sheep)
851 - Flood
852 - Flannel
853 - Flamingo
854 - Flare
855 - Fuel oil
856 - Flesh
857 - Volcano
858 - velvet
859 - Flap
860 - Fishes, vichyssoise
861 - Fishtail
862 – Fashion (show)
863 - Fish mouth
864 - Voucher
865 - Fish oil

866 - Fish jaw

867 - Fishhook

868 - half-shaved

869 - Fishbowl

870 - Figs,

871 - Factory, avocado

872 - Afghan

873 - Vacuum

874 - Foghorn

875 - Focal

876 - Vacation

877 - Half-cocked (gun)

878 - ivy-covered

879 - Fig bowl

880 – Fives (High Fives)

881 - Five toes

882 - View finder

883 - Five men

884 - Favor (party)

885 - half-oval

886 - Five shoes

887 – Five Kids

888 - Five fingers

889 - Five pins (bowling)

890 - Fobs (watch)

891 - Half a bat (baseball)

892 - half pint (ice cream)

893 - Fob maker

(Watch maker)

894 - Fabric

895 - Feeble (old man)

896 - Ivy bush

897 - Halfback (football)

898 - half-paved

899 - Half bib

900 - Buses, bosses

901 - Pastor

902 - Bison

903 - Pacemaker

904 - Pacer

905 - Pussy willow

906 - Pasture

907 - Bicycle

908 - Pacifier

909 - Baseball

910 - Beads

911 - Potato

912 - Baton

913 - Badminton

914 - Battery

915 - Pedal

916 - Beautician

917 - Bodyguard

918 – Boat Full

919 - Bat boy,

920 - Pencil

921 - Bayonet

922 - Banana

923 - Panama

(Canal or hat)

924 - Pioneer

925 - Panel

926 - Pawnshop, poncho, Banjo

927 - Pancake, pin cushion, Bank

928 - Pinfish, bonfire, Bowie Knife

929 - Pinball

930 - Beams

931 - Beamed (ceiling)

932 - Pimento

933 - Boom man (crane Operator)

934 - Boomerang

935 - Palm oil

936 - Bombshell

937 - Pomegranate

938 - Pamphlet

939 - Bambi

940 - Purse

941 – Pirate

942 - Piranha

943 - Barmaid

944 - Prayer

945 - Pearl

946 - Brush

947 - Brick

948 - Perfume

949 - Barbecue

950 - Pills

951 - Bullet

952 - Balloon

953 - Palomino

954 – Polar (bear)

955 - Pool hall

956 – Blue Jay

957 - Pelican

958 - Billfold

959 – Pallbearer

960 - Badges,

961 - Poached (Eggs)

962 - Pageant

963 - Pajamas

964 - Pusher (drugs)

965 - Pugilist

966 - Beach shoe (sandals)

967 - Paycheck

968 - Pitchfork

969 - Bishop

970 - Pigskin

971 - Picket

972 - Bacon

973 – Pac-Man

974 - Packer

975 - Pickle

976 - Bookshelf

977 - Peacock

978 - pick-off (baseball)	983 - Pavement	990 - Bobsled	997 - Popcorn
979 - Bagpipe	984 - Beaver	991 - Puppet	998 - baby face
980 - Beehives	985 - Buffalo	992 - Baboon	999 - Baby bib
981 - Beef tongue	986 – Beef Jerky	993 - Pipe man	1,000 - Diseases
982 - Bouffant (hair style)	987 - Bifocals	994 - Pepper	
	988 - Beef feeder	995 - Bible	
	989 - Beef burger	996 - pea patch	

This list is more for reference. I have been teaching memory seminars for two decades now and I am one of only a handful of people that I know who has memorized this list. If you chose to do so...Good on you! On the other hand, pictures for numbers 1-100 will be great for most applications.

day 18

Memorizing the Presidents

Welcome back to Day 18. How are you? Are you memorizing a 100-digit number yet? Well, probably not. Not right now, but I'm sure you are well on your way. Remember, you will just need 50 files to accomplish this feat. We are going to spend the next few days working on names and faces. Names and faces are probably one of the most rewarding aspects of memory training. Dale Carnegie's book, How To Win Friends And Influence People is one of the bestselling books of all time. In that book, Dale Carnegie discovered two important facts. But the first fact that Dale Carnegie discovered is that everyone's favorite subject is actually themselves. The second fact that Dale Carnegie discovered is that the sweetest sound to a person's ear, universally, in any language is the sound of their own name.

Now, be honest with me. Knowing that everybody's favorite subject is themselves and the sweetest sound to the ear is a person's own name, how many times have you been introduced to someone and as soon as that handshake breaks, boom, the name drops to the floor. It happens to everyone. It is very embarrassing. However, it happens to all of us. When you recall someone's name, you have just set yourself apart from the rest of the group in their mind. You have made a distinction between you and the others. The next question is, well, great, Ronnie, but how do you do it? Good question. I'm glad that you asked.

What are the five things that we need to recall anything? Focus, Location, code, action and Review. We utilize this knowledge to recall names, also. People's faces are actually the file. The code we use is the picture, and that picture is determined by the name.

We are going to have a memory test and this actually will help us with name memory. Your goal is to memorize this list of words below. Don't spend more than ten minutes memorizing it and see if you can memorize it faster than that. There are 44 words so you decide BEFORE you start which 44 files you are going to use.

1.) Washing Machine
2.) A Dam
3.) Chef cooking the sun
4.) Medicine
5.) Man in a row boat
6.) A Dam and Cue Balls
7.) Car jack
8.) Van on fire
9.) Hair
10.) Tie
11.) Polka dots
12.) Tailor
13.) Filling up a glass more
14.) Ear ring
15.) Blue Cannon
16.) Beard
17.) Ants drawing
18.) College Campus
19.) Fog, mist or Haze
20.) Garfield the cat
21.) Author
22.) City of Cleveland
23.) Benji the Walt Disney Dog
24.) City of Cleveland

25.) Mount McKinnely (in Alaska)

26.) Roses

27.) Raft

28.) Wilson tennis ball

29.) Hard surface

30.) Cooler

31.) Vacuum cleaner

32.) Roses

33.) Man telling truth

34.) Eyeball

35.) Ken doll (Barbie and Barbie)

36.) Airplane 'landing'

37.) Gate with water rushing through it

38.) Ford truck

39.) Peanut Butter

40.) Jelly Beans

41.) Bushes

42.) Lint

43.) Bushes

44.) Bahamas

There you have it. Now number 1-44 and see how many words that you recall. Remember the answer doesn't come to mind right away skip it and continue. Don't get slowed down with the ones that you don't recall. Finish the ones that you do know and then return to the ones that you initially missed.

So what do you think we just memorized? Well, we were talking about names so if you guessed **44** names then you are correct! But let's take it one step further, these are important names! They are the names of the **44** Presidents of The United States! Many students will spend days or weeks memorizing the presidents of the United States and you did it in only MINUTES!

Here are the answers:

1.) Washing Machine = Washington

2.) A Dam = Adams

3.) Chef cooking the sun = Jefferson (Chef Sun)

4.) Medicine = Madison

5.) Man in a row boat = Monroe

6.) A Dam and Cue Balls = Q. Adams

7.) Car jack = Jackson

8.) Van on fire = Van Buren (Van burning)

9.) Hair = Harrison

10.) Tie = Tyler

11.) Polka dots = Polk

12.) Tailor = Taylor

13.) Filling up a glass more = Fillmore

14.) Ear ring = Pierce (ear pierced to get an ear ring)

15.) Blue Cannon = Buchanan

16.) Beard = Abe Lincoln

17.) Ants drawing = Andrew (Johnson)

18.) College Campus = Grant (college grant)

19.) Fog, mist or Haze = Hayes

20.) Garfield the cat = Garfield

21.) Author = Arthur

22.) City of Cleveland = Cleveland

23.) Benji the Walt Disney Dog = Benjamin (Harrison)

24.) City of Cleveland = Cleveland

25.) Mount McKinely (in Alaska) = McKinley

26.) Roses = Roosevelt

27.) Raft = Taft

28.) Wilson tennis ball = Wilson

29.) Hard surface = Harding

30.) Cooler = Coolidge

31.) Vacuum cleaner = Hoover

32.) Roses = Franklin Roosevelt

33.) Man telling truth = Truman

34.) Eyeball = Eisenhower

35.) Ken doll (Barbie and Barbie) = Kennedy

36.) Airplane 'landing' = Lyndon (landing) Johnson

37.) Gate with water rushing through it = Nixon (Water Gate)

38.) Ford truck = Ford

39.) Peanut Butter = Jimmy Carter (His family was in the peanut business)

40.) Jelly Beans = Reagan (his favorite candy)

41.) Bushes = Bush

42.) Lint = Clinton

43.) Bushes = Bush

44.) Bahamas = Obama

There you have it! The 44 presidents!

Now, let's go back to names and faces. The five things that you need to recall a name is focus, location, a code, action and review. All we are going to focus on today is the code or turning names into pictures. We will concentrate on the others tomorrow and the next day. So, knowing that every name must be a picture to recall it, let's see what we have. And, yes, everyone I meet, I have a picture for their name. I met a gentleman today. He said, "Ronnie, I never forget a face, but I'm terrible with names." The reason for that is you see the face but you don't see the name. It is abstract to you. In order to recall a name, you have to see it, just like you saw the face.

How many times have you been out and you see someone you know but you don't know where you know them from? Then they walk up to you and they say, "Hey, Ronnie, how are you?" And you say, "Good!" and you wish you could recall their name. Then two hours later, when you're driving home, the name pops up in your head. What does that prove? Well, actually it proves a couple of things. Number one, we recall faces better than names because we see the face and not the name. The second thing that it teaches us is that our mind never actually forgets a name. Accessing and retrieving the name is the difficulty. The name is up there, but getting to it when we need it is the problem. So, let's use this knowledge to our benefit.

Now, at this point, people always say to me, wait a minute, Ronnie. Are you telling me that every time I meet someone, I'm going to have to go through this whole process and turn their name into a picture? My answer to that is, 'no.' Then they get a confused look on their face. The first time that you meet someone, the first time you meet a Ronnie, a Michelle, an Eric, an Allen, or a Debbie, you'll have to turn the name into a picture. However, the next time you meet Ronnie, Michelle, Eric, or Allen, the work is already done. You will have the picture already made. You have already done it, because you did it the first time. So, in review of today's lesson, let's focus on what we just did. We took 44 names and turned them into pictures. Today, when I meet people, I am not turning their names into pictures. For the most part, I already have the names. I'm just sticking their names on the locations or files that I have established.

day 19

Names and Faces

Hey, it's Day 19. Are you ready to advance to the next level of names memory? At this point, you understand that to recall someone's name, you have to see their name just as you see their face. Your mind remembers pictures. You have heard the saying that the picture is worth a thousand words? In this case, it is just worth one word. But that word is the sweetest sound to a person's ear.

Now that we have worked on turning names into pictures, let's focus on where we are going to store the code or where we are going to store the person's name. The location, of course, is the person's face. When you meet someone whether you are doing this consciously or subconsciously, you are doing it. When you meet someone, you look at their face and you notice certain features. For example, if you met Jay Leno, you would notice his outstanding facial feature. What would it be? Perhaps the chin. What about David Letterman? Maybe the gap in his teeth. What about Telly Savalas? Well, his head is bald. If you meet Abraham Lincoln, his beard would be his outstanding feature. Most everyone has something on their face that draws your attention. Even the most beautiful person has beautiful eyes that draw your attention, or perhaps their lip, or mouth, or nose or eye brows. Next you will see 15 faces and on each one of these faces, we are going to choose an outstanding feature.

Let's look at number one face together. We will pretend that we are
meeting this individual for the first time. The outstanding feature we

are going to choose on this face is the bushy eye brows. So, picture number one as Mr. Eyebrows. Now, don't write the name in the guidebook just yet. We are going to do that later. Just concentrate on the faces for now. Say hello to Mr. Eyebrows. Now, on to face number two. On this lady's face, make the file her cheekbones. Say hello to Miss Cheekbones. Go back and review Mr. Eyebrows, now say hello to Miss Cheekbones. Number three, let's call this gentleman Mr. Beard, because he has a beard and that is our file. Look at him and say, "Hello, Mr. Beard." Face number four, let's call this face Miss Eyes because of her large eyes. Number four is Miss Eyes because of her large eyes. Say hello to Miss Eyes. Number five is mustache. Number five is Mr. Mustache. Go back and review one through five. Review one through five. What was one, number two, number three, number four and five?

Now we are on number six. This call this guy Mr. Forehead because of his high forehead. Number seven, let's call this face Mr. Ears because of his large ears. Number seven is Mr. Ears because of his large ears. Real quick, go back and review number six, number five, number four, number three, number two, and one. Now we are on number eight. Let's make number eight Miss Lips because of her full lips. Number eight is Miss Lips because of her full lips. Look at number four. What was this person's name? Number nine, what do you think we will call this person? How about Miss Mole for the mole on her face. Miss mole is our ninth face. Here, we are on number ten. Look at this face. Let's call this face Mr. Glasses because of his glasses. Now, it is important not to use sunglasses or reading glasses because they may not have them on the next time you see them. However, if they look to be permanent and glasses are terrific, they definitely distinguish a face. Remember the ones before. Review the ones before. Look at face number one. Look at face number two, number three, number four and number five.

How about number six, number seven, number eight, number nine and ten? Ok, let's look at the next face and let's call this face Mr. Scar for the scar on his cheek. Mr. Scar. Say hello to Mr. Scar. Number 12, look at the face and call her Miss Teeth. Look at her pretty teeth and smile. Number 13, let's call this face Mr. Wrinkle for the wrinkles on his face. Number 14, call this face Mr. Dimple for the dimple on his chin. Dimples on the chin are safe to use. Sometimes, dimples on a face can only be seen when a person smiles and those are dangerous because they may not be smiling when you see them the next time. The last one, number 15, let's call this face Mr. Nose for his large nose. Mr. Nose is number 15. Look back real quick and review the ones before. What we are going to do right now is going to go back and write the names we have just given the people in the space provided below their picture. So write the names.

How did you do? Did you get all the new names? I think that you will find this pretty successful. Now you say, "Sure, Ronnie, I was able to do that, but the problem is that this is not the person's real name." You're right. If you can do this, then you are not going to have any problem recalling their name. So far, you understand to recall a person's name, you must turn their name into a picture which is actually what we covered yesterday. The second thing you need to do is observe the face and pick a distinguishing feature. These two ingredients are going to work in tandem when you recall a name. We will work tomorrow on how to put these two items together. However, do not move to Day 20 unless you understand everything we have talked about today. So, we have come to a conclusion here on Day 19.

day 20

Names and Faces

The ability to recall a person's name will light up their eyes. It makes people feel so important! I can't tell you how many times I've been tapped on the shoulder in line for a movie in Dallas and someone will say, "Ok, Mr. Memory, what's my name now?" About 70% of the time I can recall their name. What's more important, about 70% of the time, they will recall my name. Why? I'm nothing different or special over anyone else. The only thing that I did was when I left, I called them by their name. That is what differentiated me in their mind. It obligates people to recall you when you recall them.

We have already established the location is the person's face, and that is why we chose a facial feature. The next thing that we established was that the code was the name turned into a picture. And now, we're up to the next step- the action where we put the two together. Do you recall on Day 18 when we turned names into pictures and then filed them to our house files? Recalling a name works the same way; except that the difference is instead of filing the name to a piece of furniture, we're filing it to a face. There is absolutely no difference.

Looking at these faces we are now going to memorize the names with the face:

I'm going to give you two pictures to file to each person's face. Take these pictures and then file them to the entire face. However, the action should be centered around or focused on the person's outstanding feature. That was the purpose of picking it out. Let's look at the face for number one. Now, do not write anything down until you are instructed to do so. Remember this is a memory program. Here we go! This person's name is John Webster. First turn this name into a picture. The picture for John is a toilet and Webster is from Webster's Dictionary. Looking at a picture, number one, we are going to file a toilet and a dictionary to his eye brows. This is just like we did to our house files, the only difference is that we filed it to someone's face.

Now, the second face. This person's name is Debbie Wayne. The picture for Debbie is dead bee and the picture for Wayne is rain. Every time you meet a Debbie, the picture is a dead bee, and the picture for Wayne is always rain. Now, let's focus on her facial file. We see that it was her cheekbones. As you look at her picture, begin to notice that there is a dead bee on each of her cheekbones and is being showered by rain. Perhaps you just met this woman in a social situation and you see this dead bee and rain on her face. Remember to focus the action around her cheekbones. The next time you see her cheekbones, there will be the brain trigger. Review number one. What was his name? Review the picture. Her name? Debbie Wayne.

Number three. This gentleman's name is Paul Russ. Every Paul is a basketball and every Russ is rust. As we decided yesterday, our file for this gentleman is his beard. So, as you look at this man's face, visualize yourself dribbling a basketball made out of rust on his beard. Again, look at the beard and visualize a basketball made out of rust being dribbled on his beard. Use all your senses. Imagine the taste, the smell, and feel the basketball made out of rust. His name is Paul Russ.

Number four. This lady's name is Ann Green. The picture for Ann is ants and the picture for green is green! The file for this woman is her eyes, so we are going to file ants in her eyes and they are all green. Now, remember that your pictures for these things need to be larger than life. Make the ants huge, and they are crawling around in her eyes and they're green. Maybe they're crawling out of her eyes, and they come out and they come to get you. Now, that would be somewhat of a gross picture, but guess what? You won't soon forget it. So file ants and green to your file, and it's Ann Green. Review the ones before.

Number five. What is your file? That's right, your file is the mustache. This gentleman's file is a mustache and his name is Chris Gordon. The picture for Chris is a cross and the picture for Gordon is a garden. So look at this man. You notice that his mustache is really a garden and it is growing nothing but crosses! That is a picture! A garden that is growing nothing but crosses. Again, his name is Chris Gordon. Cross for Chris and garden for Gordon.

Number six, his file is the high forehead. His name is Mark Reeves. Every Mark is a marker, like the one you write with, and Reeves is a reef, like the Great Barrier Reef or a coral reef. On this gentleman's forehead, visualize a marker drawing a reef on his forehead. Again, draw a coral reef on this gentleman's head with a marker. This gentleman's name is Mark Reeves. Mark Reeves. Look at his picture and visualize the image that we just described.

Number seven. What was the file? It was ears. This gentleman's name is Steve Light. Every Steve is a stove and every Light is a light bulb. We said that his ears are the file, so we are going to put his large ears in the stove. We are cooking his ears and then the light bulb goes off and tells us that the cooking is done. Remember, don't just say it, see it. Saying it does little, but seeing it does everything.

Number eight, what is the file? The file for this one is full lips. The lady's name is Margaret and her last name is Sanders. The picture for Margaret is a margarita and the picture for Sanders is a sander. As you observe this woman's face, you notice she is drinking a margarita that is nothing but sand. Perhaps the sand is all over her lips and her teeth, and she smiles and she drinks the sand margarita.

Number nine. This lady's name is Elizabeth Smith. The picture for Elizabeth is a lizard with bad breath, and the picture for Smith is always a blacksmith iron. As you look at the picture of this lady, a lizard with really bad breath comes to sit on her mole. You, not liking lizards, decide to kill it with a blacksmith's iron. So, look at her picture and see yourself branding this lizard with a blacksmith's branding iron.

Number ten. We have decided that on his face the file was going to be his glasses, right? His name is Al Cash. Every Al, an owl, and a Cash is, of course, money. So, the pictures that we are going to put on his face are an owl and money. Look at this picture and see an owl in his glasses, and the owl is made out of money. Every time he opens his mouth to hoot, a quarter comes out! Look at the picture and visualize this taking place on his glasses. Now, owl is for the name, Al. And money is for the last name, Cash. Say hello to Al Cash. Go back and review the ones from before. See the picture and then recall what the name stood for. Number one, number two, three, four, five, six, seven, eight, nine and number ten. Review them all.

This is how you memorize names. Go back now and see how many of the names that you can recall.

So, how did you do? Did you get all of them? I bet you did pretty well. If you were able to see these pictures, then it wasn't difficult at all. If you didn't see the picture, then that was a challenge. If you were able to recall the picture but not the name, don't worry. These pictures were mine. In real life, you will be creating the pictures that will be representing the names, so you are not going to have a problem recalling what the picture stood for. It will be obvious to you because it was your picture.

Let's grade your test real quick before we wrap it up for today. Number one was John Webster. Number two was Debbie Wayne. Three was Paul Russ. Four is Ann Green. Five is Chris Gordon. Six is Mark Reeves. Seven is Steve Light. Eight is Margaret Sanders. Nine is Elizabeth Smith. And ten was, of course, Al Cash. There you have it. Ten names and ten pictures and ten faces.

In real life, it's no different than this process. Always repeat the person's name in the conversation. When I'm going home after a meeting with someone, I'll review their name in their facial files, and then I will even review it a few days later. It is a little bit of work, you better believe it! However, is it worth it? When you see a person six months after you have met them and you recall their name, then you have just placed yourself in a very select category. You have made them feel good about themselves, and you have just gone from the level of acquaintance to friend. And, believe me, it's worth every ounce of effort, and keep this in mind. When I'm meeting people today, I'm not having to ask myself, "What is the picture for this person's name?" You already are going to have the pictures for every Robert. Once you do it, it's done. For every Lisa, you do it once. For every John, once, and so on. Initially, this system will take a little bit of work to build up the Encyclopedia of names. However, once the Encyclopedia of Names is built up, this is as easy as one, two, three.

The challenge that I lay down for you is this. Every time you meet a person over the next three to four weeks turn their name into a picture. If you are at the movie theatre, bank, ATM machine, grocery store, church, school, gas station or at an office turn the name of the person that you meet into a picture. When you meet a Steve ask yourself, 'What is a picture for Steve?' Once you determine what it is then use that picture for every Steve. My picture for Steve is a stove. So EVERYTIME I meet a Steve I see a stove. Do not and I repeat DO NOT use Stove one day and then the next time you meet a Steve create a different picture for Steve. This will only complicate the process.

Here are a few examples:

Karen = Carrot
Michelle = Missle
Wendi = Wind
Kyle = Tile
Hilary = Hill of Trees
Lisa = Mona Lisa
Rick = Brick

Don = Sunrise
Dave = Cave
David = Divot
Tom = Tomcat
Abby = A bee
Paul = Ball
Crystal = Crystal
Nancy = Nun eating seeds
Candy = Candy
Dan = Pan
Linda = Window

day 21

Names and Faces

The keys to remember when meeting someone are focus on their face and distinguishing features. Then take their name and turn it into a picture. Then with action, tie that picture to the face. We are going to go through the same drill as we did on Day 20. This time, we are just going to meet 5 people. Actually, you have already met these people before. They are left over from Day 19. You have their outstanding facial features, now you just need their name. Remember that their whole face is actually where you store the name. The outstanding facial feature is where you put the picture on where it's focused.

This is Miss Teeth, remember her? Her name is Judy Rose. The picture for Judy is chewing tea and the picture for Rose is a rose. So, look at the picture and at her teeth. The picture is her chewing tea bags for Judy. Remember to incorporate all your senses. See it, hear it, taste it. You have chewing tea for Judy, now maybe a rose in her hair or in her mouth. After she chews the tea, she chews the rose to get the taste out of her mouth.

Number two. This is Mr. Scar. His name is Brian Nichols. The picture for Brian is a brain and the picture for Nichols is nickels, money, like nickels you spend. So, let's look at the picture and specifically the scar. Act as if this is a real person you are meeting for the first time. As you are looking at the scar, you see a brain poking out of the scar. You grab some nickels and you cover up the exposed brain. Wow! You're covering up his exposed brain with nickels!

The next face is Mr. Wrinkle. His name is Dan Frog. Every Dan is a pan, like a pan you cook with and, of course, Frog is a frog. Look at Mr. Wrinkle and on his face is a pan and cooking in the pan is a frog. His face is actually a stove that is cooking frogs. As you are talking to him, maybe you reach down in the pan and you decide to have some frog legs.

The next one is Mr. Dimple because of the dimple in his chin. His name is Craig Robbins. For every Craig is a keg and every Robbins is the bird, a robin. So, let's look at this gentleman and resting on his chin is a keg and several robins have gathered around and are drinking out of the keg. This gentleman is actually a walking bird feeder. Every time you saw him, he had a swarm of robins around him feeding off the keg on his chin, you'd never forget it! You'd tell everybody about it.

The last gentleman is Mr. Nose. And his name is Tom Lewis. Every Tom is a tom cat and every Lewis is a loose s. Moving all around the gentleman's nose is a loose s. It's running around like crazy! Can you guess what's chasing the s? Sure, I bet you can, a cat, a tom cat to be precise.

This should be getting a little bit clearer and easier. I hope that you are following along just fine. Is this process that you're going through whenever you meet a person? The answer to that question is absolutely yes. Don't let that discourage you. This is an aspect of memory training that requires a little bit of effort. However, if it didn't require effort, it wouldn't be worth it. Also, remember that the effort is at the beginning. The work is going to be building up an Encyclopedia of names. The first time ever that I spoke to a company as a memory training speaker, I only called on three people because I only wanted to be responsible to retain three names. As I got more confident in the system, I slowly worked my way up. Today, it is no big deal for me to meet fifty people in thirty minutes and recall their names. However, I did not start there and you will not either. Don't get discouraged because you can't recall five people right now. You are going to meet people today and tomorrow anyway. So turn their name into a picture. If you have to meet them anyway, then turn their name into a picture. Just give it a try. I think you'll be impressed, and remember, I review the name on the way home after I meet someone and even a few days later. You have to if you want to cement it in.

day 22

Fun Memory Demonstrations

Today is going to be a fun day. I'm going to teach you some memory games or stunts you can play with your friends. These are neat demonstrations of a trained memory. There are several purposes that these games have. Number one, you get to have some fun. Number two, you get to practice the system. And number 3, people will get to ask you how you did it! And you will get the privilege of teaching them the system.

The first demonstration is actually one I saw a memory expert demonstrate on the Tonight Show with Johnny Carson. It got quite a reaction. However, it was actually very simple. For this demonstration, the memory expert used 50 files. Johnny handed him a magazine and gave him a few minutes to look at it while Johnny went on with the show. When they came back to the memory expert, Johnny took the magazine back and said, "What did page 23 talk about?" The expert said, "The article was talking about motorcycles." Everyone applauded. He said, "Ok, Mr. Bigshot, what about page 47?" He said, "That was the ad about the trip to Hawaii." This blew everyone away. However, with a little bit of understanding in memory training, we could figure out what he was doing. He glanced at every page, got the general idea, turned it into a picture, then filed that to his file. He did this with 50 files and that was pretty easy, actually. However, it got quite a reaction and it should get a reaction if you do it as a demonstration. That is a fun one.

Another fun memory stunt is to memorize the serial numbers on dollar bills. Have everyone hand you a dollar bill. To do this, you must understand phonics and have pictures for two digit numbers. Look at the serial numbers and then file them to your house files. You must also turn the letters into pictures. A is ax, b is a bicycle, c is a computer, d is a drum and so on. You have five rooms in your files. Make each room dedicated to a bill. File the pictures to your files and you should amaze everyone. Now, don't bet money when you do these stunts because your friends probably won't be your friends for long if you take money from them.

Here's another neat stunt. Write out 50 to 100 numbers on a sheet of paper. Give the paper to a friend and have them circle five numbers. Then, tell him to call out all the numbers that he has on his paper except the ones he circled. Tell him to do this in random order. As he is doing this, you are mutilating the file he is calling out. Maybe you are destroying it or throwing water on it or setting it on fire. It really doesn't matter what you do, just change it up somehow. Then, when he gets done, go through your files and the five that you have done nothing to are the ones that he circled. This makes the hair stand up on the back of people's neck. Quite a feat!

Here's another fun one. Have you ever wanted to learn the calendar for an entire year? Well, it's actually easier than you think. It is going to take just 12 files and each file represents a month of the year. For example, January is represented by a baby. February is represented by Cupid. March is soldiers marching. April is an umbrella. May is flowers. June is a June bug. July is fire crackers. August is the sun. September is a school. October is a pumpkin. November is a turkey. And December is a Christmas tree. The next item of business is to determine the first Sunday of every month. For example, if the first Sunday in January is the fifth, you will file a star to baby. You use the pencil list and the picture from their file to your 12 month files. Then when someone asks you, "What day of the week is the 23rd of January?" You say, well, that's a Thursday. All you have to do is count from the first Sunday by sevens until you get to the week which the day in question falls on. If it is one number away, you know it is Monday. Two days away, it is Tuesday, three days away it is Wednesday, four is Thursday, five is Friday and six is Saturday. All you have to do is learn the first Sunday of all 12 months and you have a neat little demonstration that you can do. This one is more than just a memory stunt. You will actually be able to use this to help you in your life.

When you're sitting in a board meeting and someone says, "Let's meet again on the 18th of June," you can say, "That is no good because that's a Sunday." Everyone thinks, did he memorize the whole calendar? No. But they never pass up an opportunity to demonstrate the system.

Other memory games can be just as fun. Have someone give you items and file them to your files. People love this! I encourage you to teach the system after you do this demo. Don't hog the spotlight. People will appreciate your willingness to share. These are just some games. There are many more. If you think of some on your own, send me a letter or email. I always like to have fun with this system.

day 23

Memorizing a Deck of Cards

This is one of my favorite memory demonstrations! I love to get a deck of cards and shuffle them up and then race through them in a little over a minute and hand the deck to someone and I will call off the cards in order as they flip them over! POWERFUL and FUN!

There are many systems out there to memorize a deck of cards but the one I am going to describe below is incredibly powerful and is used by memory experts all over the world to memorize a deck of cards in under 27 seconds! Yes, you read that right! Ben Pridmore of the United Kingdom has memorized a deck of cards in 26.2 seconds! Dominic O'Brien has memorized 54 decks (2808 cards) and David Farrow 59 decks (3068)! There systems may not be exactly like the one I will describe below but it is pretty close.

When I memorize a deck of cards I am memorizing 3 cards at a time. Remember earlier when we talked about character/action/object for numbers. Well, I also have character/action/object for every card. There are many ways that you can do this. Personally this is how I have done it.

I assigned a number to every card:

Spades are represented by the numbers 2-14. The two of spades equals the number two in my mind. The ten of spades equals the number ten in my mind. Jack = 11, Queen = 12, King = 13 and Ace = 14

Hearts are represented by the numbers 22-34. The two of hearts equals number 22 in my mind. The ten of hearts equals number 30. Jack = 31, Queen = 32, King = 33 and Ace = 34

Diamonds are represented by the numbers 42-54. The two of diamonds equals the number 42 in my mind. The ten of diamonds equals the number 50. Jack = 51, Queen = 52, King = 53 and Ace = 54.

Clubs are represented by the numbers 60-74 in my mind. The two of clubs equals the number 62. The ten of clubs equals the number 70. Jack = 71, Queen = 72, King = 73 and Ace = 74

The next step is to think of a person that goes with each number. 33 could be your mom because using the phonics we discovered before three is 'muh'. 33 = mom. What does your mom like to do? Maybe cook? So the action would be cooking and the object would be a frying pan. The character/action/object for you would be mom cooking in a pan. This all represents the number 33 for you and more importantly the King of Hearts.

You can create the characters (people) this way using numbers and phonics. I like this method because it kills two birds with one stone. You are also creating pictures for numbers this way! You can create your own rules. I have a friend named Kristen Payne and she represents the number 79 for me because 79 is 'Kuh' and 'Puh'. Thus we have the initials K.P. But I don't always use the initials, my picture for 65 is a friend of mine named Ashley. Because six is 'shuh' and five is 'luh'. So 65 is Ashley for me. You are going to have to develop your own method.

Another way to create the character/action/object is you could create pictures based on something like this:

Every card in the hearts suit is someone that you love

Every card in the club suit is someone that is famous

Every card in the spades suit is someone you work with

Every card in the diamond suit is someone rich.

Then after you have created the person/character for each card then you create an action and object that would go with that card. For example if Albert Einstein becomes one of your characters then your action might be experimenting and the object might be a test tube.

Now, hopefully this makes sense and you are able to create a character/action/object for each card.

Then you start memorizing!

You take the first three cards and they are King of Hearts, Ace of Spades and Jack of Diamonds. You create a quick story using the character for the first card, the action for the second card and the object for the third card. You then file this to your first file. You do this with 17 files and then on the 18ᵗʰ file you just put one character. After you have done this you mentally go back through your files and on each file you should have a character/action/object. The character is the first card, the action is the second card and the object is the third card.

There you have it! You now know how the memory experts memorize a deck of cards in less than a minute. Practice this method until you get really good and then I hope to see you at a championship soon!

day 24

Memorizing Scripture

Do you recall the pencil list? Let's review it together. Number one is a pencil because it looks like a number one. Number two is a sink because it has two options, on and off. Number three is a ring for three-ring circus. Number four is a track, four times around is a mile. Number five is a star because it has five points. Number six is a bullet, a six shooter, six feet under. Number seven is dice, lucky seven, opposite sides always equal seven. Number eight is an hourglass shaped like an eight. Number nine is a baseball, nine players, nine innings. Number ten is fingers, ten fingers, ten toes.

Number 11 is a goal post, 11 players on a team, shaped like an 11. Number 12 is eggs, a dozen eggs. Number 13, well that was flag, 13 stars, 13 stripes, 13original colonies. Number 14, what was that? Necklace, 14 karat gold, 14 Valentine's Day, February 14. How about 15, remember that one? It was paycheck, the first and the 15th you get paid. Number 16, what was it? You got car, right? Sixteen, you get your driver's license. Number 17, what is it? Magazine. There's a magazine called Seventeen. Number 18, what was it? Soldier, remember 18, you register for the draft? Number 19, what was that? Golf clubs, you better believe it. The 19th hole. And number 20 is a shotgun. Why? Twenty gauge shotgun. Remember this list was created by using basic association, however, this is also a file system because there is more than one of them and they go in a logical order.

There are 20 files. It also demonstrated to us what basic association is. This is a list that could be used to file anything, and remember that whatever you want to recall, you have to turn into a picture. That is the code, the hard drive that your mind thinks in. If you want to recall lines of poetry or a quote, remember all you have to do is get a general idea and turn it into a picture, and then file that file to your pencil list. There are 20 files that had unlimited possibilities. Now we may have another file system that we want to keep fresh in your minds, and that is our skeleton files. This is a ten-file file system and works great for a lot of different possibilities.

I taught a seminar in New Orleans last year. Before it was my turn to speak, the company offered $50 to anyone who could say the mission statement. One gentleman out of the whole company could say it. I stood up and I said, "How many of you think I could teach you the mission statement forwards, backwards, in and out of order, or by number in less than seven minutes?" No one believed me. However, they were all eager with anticipation. Everyone wanted to be able to do it. We broke their mission statement down into ten lines and each one of those lines we turned into a picture and then simply filed those to our skeleton files. In just a few short minutes, we had memorized their mission statement and everyone was amazed. I bring up this story for this reason.

Sometimes when you are memorizing information using this system, you may think to yourself, "This is no big deal. This isn't that hard." If that is what you are thinking, then you're right. It isn't hard because we are approaching it from the correct angle the first time. If we are using rote memorization first and then this system as the company in New Orleans, you would see the difference. So, keep in mind that when someone gives me a list of 15 to 25 words and I memorize it forwards and backwards, and by number, it blows them away. You have seen that demo and that is why you taking this program most likely. If that is true, remember this. You were impressed with the results, not the process. Just because you know the process, do not let that change the fact that this is a very impressive demonstration.

Now, let's review our skeleton files. They are number one is top, two is nose, three is nose, four is ribs, five is liver, six is joint, seven is cap, eight is fibula, nine is ball and ten is sand. Now, these are our files. I recently did a program in Norfolk, Virginia where I was asked to teach a group the Ten Commandments, and they wanted to know them forwards and backwards, and by number. I taught them the skeleton files and then we learned the Ten Commandments using the skeleton files.

Let's do this together. What is your file? It is top. The First Commandment is to have no other gods. We must turn that phrase into a picture. Make a picture in your mind of what have no other gods before represents to you. Some people it may be money, power, fame, or something that they put as the ultimate in their life that is their god. When you hear the verse, have no other gods before me, file that picture to your top.

Number two, what is your file? It is nose. The Second Commandment says you shall not make a graven image. Let's focus on two words, graven and image and file a tombstone to your nose. Do you see the correlation? Tombstone marks a grave? Touch your nose right now with your finger and imagine a tombstone crushing your finger and your nose.

Number three is your mouth, and the Third Commandment is not take the name of the Lord in vain. Your file is mouth. Open your mouth really wide and imagine you are writing with a marker your name all over your teeth. Every time you smile, you have your name written all over your teeth. For example, my teeth say Ronnie all over them.

Now, what is your number four file? It's your ribs. The Fourth Commandment is to keep the Sabbath holy. The substitute picture for Sabbath is a bath. Sabbath is a bath. File your ribs getting a bath.

The next file is your liver. The Fifth Commandment is honor your father and mother. Close your eyes and see a picture of your mother and father in your mind. Now take that picture and with action, file it to your liver. Maybe you see your mom and your dad standing on your liver, or they are on the inside and they are trying to get out.

Number six, what is your file? It is your joint. The Sixth Commandment is you shall not murder. Have someone sticking a knife into your hip joint. This is the verse, thou shall not murder.

Number seven, what is your file? It's your cap, right? The number Seven Commandment is thou shall not commit adultery. File a tree growing out of your kneecap and a doll is hanging on the tree. A doll on a tree, adultery.

Number eight, what is your file? It is the fibula. The Eighth Commandment is you shall not steal. What do you think of when I say steal? Is it the act of stealing something or a steel bar, or is it Superman because he's the man of steel. For the purposes of this, let's use Superman. Look down at your fibula, and Superman lands there and is standing on your leg. You reach down and pat him on the head. You tell everyone, "Hey, look! It's the man of steel!"

Number nine, what is it? It is a ball, as in the ball of your foot. This commandment says do not bear false witness. So, let's just get a brain trigger for false. Let's file a red light bulb for false. File a red light bulb for false. Can you see a red light bulb and it's flashing, perhaps the light breaks and cuts your foot?

Number ten is sand. I want you to file a Corvette. What color do you like the best? Does it have leather seats? See it so you won't forget it. File it to sand. What does a Corvette have to do with the Tenth Commandment? Number ten says, thou shalt not covet. Covet is an abstract, but you can see Corvette. So, number ten is thou shall not covet.

Review and see how many that you recall.

How did you do? Did you get all ten? If you didn't get a perfect score, remember, and I've said this a million times, it is but of two reasons. Number one, is you didn't know your file, or number two, your action wasn't vivid enough. Most the time you will not recall an item because it is not vivid enough. That is the key to this whole system. Let's go through them one through ten and see how you did.

1.) Something that you worship
2.) Grave
3.) Writing a name
4.) Taking a bath
5.) Mother and father
6.) Knife
7.) Doll in a tree
8.) Superman
9.) Light bulb
10.) Corvette

Now, if you're saying, "Ronnie, this is good because I can remember the picture, but I'm having a hard time recalling what these items stood for." That is not a problem, not at all. The reason for that is because these are my pictures and this information is just for practice. If this was information that was important to you, and you were turning the abstracts into pictures, then you would know what the pictures stood for when the time comes. Practice these techniques with your friends. Have them give you 15 or 20, or even 30 or 50 items. File them to your files and encourage them to give them to you quickly. However, speed is not the main concern in this situation. The main concern is making sure that you understand the concepts.

day 25

Working on Speed Memory

If there is one thing that I have done that has impacted my memory more than anything in the last year it is that I have pushed my mind on the issue of speed. As I type this, just ten short months ago it took me over six minutes to memorize a deck of 52 shuffled cards! About two months ago I was down to three minutes! I was excited and I emailed my memory coach (yes I have a memory coach!). His name is David Thomas. He is a man who has had a Guinness World Record by memorizing pie to over 20,000 digits and has won the USA Memory Championship (2007) and placed very well at the World Memory Championship level (which is VERY hard to do). At any rate, I emailed him and shared my excitement of being able to memorize a deck of cards in three minutes. He commended my speed but then urged me to be able to do it in two minutes! I thought, 'Wow! He doesn't understand how I never thought I would get to three minutes!' However, I pressed on.

Ben Pridmore who is the current record holder for memorizing a deck of cards in 26.2 seconds gave me similar advice. He said, 'Don't wait until you are 100% sure that the image is in your memory. Instead, move to the next file and keep going. You will be surprised when you return to the file to discover that information is still in your memory.' Ben's philosophy was to move rapidly and trust your memory that is will store the data at a higher rate of speed.

Both Ben and David were correct. It took me eight months to go from six minutes to three minutes and then in only four weeks I was able to memorize a deck of cards in less than two minutes! Before you knew it I set a record for the fastest to memorize a deck of cards in one minute and 27 seconds on March 7th 2009!!

Learn to trust your memory more, don't feel like you make sure the image is 100% cemented in before you move on to the next item. You will be surprised at how much your memory really does recall.

A great way to work on speed memory is to get a computer program that generate random words or random numbers. I have programs such as this on my website www.ronwhitetraining.com. You can calibrate the speed for your purposes and then speed it up as you get better and better.

The average mind can read 250 words per minute and with speed reading can reach levels of 1000 words per minute or more. My good friend Howard Berg who is in the Guinness Book of World Record as the World's Fastest Reader says that the #1 thing that slows him down when reading is turning the pages!!

Train for accuracy but also remember to train for speed! Your mind will operate at incredibly fast and efficient levels if you push it!

day 26

Things To Do, Directions, Names

Once again, it is very simple, to remember anything all you need is :

1.) Focus
2.) Location
3.) Code
4.) Action
5.) Review

I want you to file your things to do list to your skeleton files today. Start with your top, always start with number one. When I'm ending each day, I will lay in my bed and I'll ask myself, "What do I have to do tomorrow?" I will then file that to my skeleton files. Whenever you go through the process in your day, use your skeleton files. Let's say you have five things to do, and someone calls you through the day and says, "Don't forget to call Tom!" Your picture for Tom is a tom cat. So, you immediately file that to your next open file. That way, throughout the day, you are always adding on. When you complete a task on your files, change the picture somehow. Set it on fire or throw water on it visualize a big red checkmark, but always use your skeleton files for a things to do list for the day. This is great to make things get done.

Now, how about directions? Have you ever been stopped and you ask somebody for directions and then you don't remember what the guy said? They'll say, "Go down to Maple Street and take a left and go two stop signs and take a right. Go to King Street and take a left and you're there." You drive away thinking, "Great!" And no sooner are you gone you can't recall what they just told you. It happens all the time. This is because right and lefts are abstract. Here is something you can do to recall directions.

Make every right, rain and every left a lamb. So when someone says, "Go down to Maple Street and take a left", file maple syrup and a lamb to your first file. Then they say, "Go two stop signs and make a right." File two stop signs and rain to your next file. Then when they say, "Go to King Street and take a left", file king's crown and a lamb to your number three file. What you're doing is simply turning abstracts into pictures. Remember that your mind thinks in pictures. That is the code your mind needs to recall. So what you are filing is pictures for abstracts.

How about this one? You go to a friend's house and you can't recall where you put your keys. You know, I do this all the time. Every time I place my keys, where I set them is my file and the picture, of course, is my keys, and the action is an explosion whenever I set my keys down. My friends don't know it, but when I go to their house, I'm exploding all of their furniture. You have a great system in your hands. You can use it to do anything as long as you put your mind to it. I want to conclude today's program by practicing some numbers and how to turn them into pictures using phonics. Let's do ten numbers, 11 through 20. Eleven would be tuh and tuh, so that is tot. Twelve would be tuh and nuh, so that is like a tin can. Number 13 would be tuh and muh, so that is time. See a clock. Number 14 is tuh and ruh, so that would be a tire. Number 15 is tuh and luh, so that would be tile. Sixteen is duh and shuh, so that is dish. Seventeen is tuh and cuh, so that is tack. Eighteen is duh and vuh, so that is dove. Nineteen is tuh and puh, so that is tap. Twenty is nuh and suh, so that is nose.

Phonics is a skill that if you master, you are going to find yourself with an unstoppable memory. When I get a phone number, I use phonics to file it to my skeleton files. Do I have a day timer for my phone numbers? Absolutely! However, I'm not in a rush to put the numbers in there. When I get a phone number, I use phonics to turn it into a picture, and then I file it away.

Here is a memory test for today. Turn the following names into picture:

Frank
Harold
Tommy
George
Blaine
Sally
Sarah
Natalie
Daniel
Rebecca
Heidi
Judy
Melissa
Missy
William
Davey
Barney
Jacob
Burt

day 27

Things To Do, Directions, Names

Well, it's Day 27. We're getting closer and closer to making sure you have an instant recall memory. Are you excited? I know I am! You have learned a lot. Feel free to go back and review any portion of this program at any time. There are many sections like the phonics and names that you need to review. Stick to the basics at first. Master them, then try the advanced stuff.

Today I want to give you some ideas for your files. Your house files can be used for product knowledge and I want to make sure you see that. You have five rooms and five files in each room. If you were an automobile sales professional, you can dedicate each room to one type of car. If you're a real estate agent, you get listings. Make each room represent an area of town and then always have five listings in each room. That way, when someone says they want a house in a specific area, and you have five listings at your mental fingertips, about that area. That is a great tool. If you are in any other kind of business, you can file procedures, or sales presentations, or steps to overcoming objections.

My family is in the furniture refinishing business, marketing to hotels and refinishing their furniture. And occasionally if I am in a town where they have a hotel they are trying to get work at, I will stop by and give a sales presentation. I don't know much about refinishing furniture, but I'll talk to the crew leader back home about what he wants me to say. I will then file that to my skeleton files, whether it be specific steps in restoring the furniture they use in their process or names of other hotels they have done in the area. I will file the information to my skeleton files and I sound extremely knowledgeable.

If you're a student, you are going to have to take notes the exact same way you have always done, I hate to break the news to you, but it's true. You still read the chapters the exact same way that you've always done. The difference is when you study, you only have to study once. You know people will always find time to do something over again, but they can never find time to do it right the first time. As a student, that is exactly what you are going to be doing with this system. Doing it right the first time.

Let's say you are studying for a history test in your first room. You could make that room the causes of the Civil War. The next room could be the key leaders or battles. Maybe the next room, some of the changes the war brought about. Perhaps you are studying for a psychology test and you make the first room their theories and ideas or Sigmund Freud. The second room could be theories and ideas of Carl Young. The third room could be five theories or ideas of B. F. Skinner. Or perhaps you could simply have a room that lists all the major psychologists. You have a lot of different options with this method, but it all comes down to location, code and action. You must be able to see what you want to recall and see it with a lot of action. That is the key to this whole system.

Now, for our activities, do you remember your city files? Review them real quick. Stop the program if you have to. Mentally file the following ten items to your city files and remember to move quickly and see creative items with a lot of action!

1.) Sun
2.) Mercury
3.) Venus

4.) Earth

5.) Mars

6.) Jupiter

7.) Saturn

8.) Uranus

9.) Neptune

10.) Pluto

You just memorized the planets in order from the sun! If you wanted you could go back and add an item to each picture. For example you could turn the miles from the sun into a picture and place that picture on top of each file as well. Then you would have two items on each file and so on. If you want to memorize sub points for something you do it using the system that we learned with the Mount Rainer story. Remember when you created that story? What if you filed Mount Rainer to your number one file? Well you would actually be filing much more than Mount Rainer to that #1 file; you would be filing almost 20 items. So, if you want to recall sub points to something you will file the initial item or word and then go back and create layers. File the second 'layer' then the third and fourth and so on. This is how you memorize sub-points!

day 28

Alphabet Files

Welcome, my friend! It is Day 28. The most important part of the program is going to be to implement it. You have 25 house files, ten skeleton files, 20 pencil files and ten city files. That is 65 items. There is no doubt in my mind that I could give you 65 words and right now you could get at least 55 of them. That is very impressive, guys. What you have is a valuable opportunity. Remember to get the best benefit from the gym, you have to go work out.

Yesterday, I met four people. Today as I was driving, I was reviewing their pictures and the names of their pictures. I met an Andrew with a goatee and I had ants drawing on a goatee. I met an Elizabeth with glasses. I had a lizard with bad breath on her glasses. I met a Paul with sideburns. He had a basketball bouncing on his sideburns. Then finally, I met a Tim with bushy eyebrows. He had a tin can on his eye brows. Did that require a little bit of thought? Yes a little bit. However, is it going to be worth it? You better believe it. Few things are more rewarding than making another person feel special and important, and that is exactly what you do when you recall their name. The same effort you put into names, you will have to consciously put into other areas of this system.

I want to show you another filing system that I have seen used before. Actually, kids really like this one. Not only is it good to use as files, but when you need to recall letters such as the letters in product codes or sequences, this system works great, and it works on the concept that you must see something to recall it. Here are 26 Alphabet files.

A = Ax	N = Net
B = Bicycle	O = Octopus
C = Computer	P = Pen
D = Drum	Q = Quilt
E = Ear	R = River
F = Fire	S = Sign
G = Grass	T = Tent
H = House	U = Umbrella
I = Igloo	V = Vase
J = Jet	W = Wine
K = Knight	X = X Ray
L = Light	Y = Yo Yo
M = Moon	Z = Zipper

Now, what are these 26 items? Good question. And the answer is, they're whatever you want them to be! If you find yourself in a situation where you see a math formula and there are letters that keep repeating, well, these 26 items give you pictures for those letters. They also give you 26 files if you choose to use them for that. This system is meant to give you a system that you can change to your own needs. Review it a couple of times, if you want, or whenever you encounter something that you feel these could be of use, come back to them. It could be great for memorizing product codes with letters in them, serial numbers that have letters in them or license plates. These items all contain letters and now you have pictures for letters!

day 29

Keep Your Motivation Up!

Welcome back! Today is Day 29. How did you like your alphabet picture? It was kind of interesting. Today I want to review with you what we have learned. You have learned a system developed by the Romans over 2,000 years ago, almost 2,500 years ago, to give speeches and presentations without notes. The Romans called this method Losa which is the Latin word for places. Guys, what we have done is establish places in your memory where we are going to store information. Remember they are places that you can see.

The pencil list has 20 files on it. Review them in your mind and in your guidebook if you have to. The skeleton file has ten files on it. They are top, nose, mouth, ribs, liver, joint, cap, fibula, ball and sand. Remember that not only are these files, but they also represent the ten primary phonetic sounds of tuh, nuh, muh, luh, juh, cuh, fuh, puh and suh. Remember using phonics we can create new word-pictures that can be used as files to help us recall something.

Our city files and our house files give us 25 plus ten files for 35 total files. You have 65 files. That should get you through most anything you need to retain. If you are a student, you are still going to have to take your notes just like you always did. You're still going to have to read the chapter and highlight the key information just like you always did. The difference will come when you go to retain it, and you now have a system and you are going to have to study once and then you'll be done! You will get it right the first time. I find it odd that people can always find something to do over, but they can rarely find time to do right the first time. This system enables you to do that. When someone gives you their phone number, immediately turn it into a picture and file it to your files. Or, if you want, use their house or their office and file a picture to that file whether it be their house or their office.

I recently had a student ask me if I could teach them to recall all 213 counties in his state. I said, "Yes!" Now that sounds somewhat overwhelming, but this is what you do when you encounter a situation like this. When you have an overwhelming amount of information to recall, look at it on paper. Most likely you will have to get it on paper anyway. Get it on paper and then decide how many files you're going to use. If you need more files, add some house or city or even phonics files. Once you have enough files, then break the task down into easy manageable steps. Deadlines for each goals. Once you do that, you will not be attempting a huge memory feat, you will be attempting several small feats and that is what this course if full of. You should be very well equipped right now to handle just about every situation that you encounter.

I would like to tell you the story of a west Texas rancher millionaire. He had a party to attract all the suitable bachelors around for his daughter. This is what we call in sales as group prospecting. The night was full of food and music and dancing. After everyone had fun, the west Texas rancher asked everyone to gather around an Olympic-size swimming pool that he had out back. He had the foresight to stock this pool with alligators and water moccasins, not very pleasant. He stood at the end of the pool and he said, "I will make an offer to the first man to dive into this pool and swim the length of it." He said. "I will offer him the choice of 3 things. Number one, he can have one million dollars in cold, hard cash, or number two, he can have 5,000 acres of my best land and number three, you could have my beautiful daughter in marriage, and gentlemen, obviously, if you take the hand of my daughter, one day all of this will be yours because one day this all will be hers." Well, no sooner had the words left his mouth, there was a splash at one end of the pool and a young man emerged at the other end and he had just set a world's record that will never be eclipsed. The rancher was so excited, he ran over and he said, "Son, I guess you want something!" He said, "Yes, sir." The rancher said, "Well, tell me, son, what is it that you want? Do you want the million dollars in cold, hard cash?" The young man said, "No, sir." He said, "Well, son, do you want the 5,000 acres of my best land?" And the young man said, "No, sir." The west Texas rancher said, "Well then, son, I'm assuming that you want the hand of my beautiful daughter in marriage." The young man said, "No, sir." The rancher was shocked! He said, "Son, if you don't want the hand of my beautiful daughter in marriage, you don't want the cash, you don't want the land, son, tell me what it is you want. What do you want?" The young man said, "I want to know the name of that dude who pushed me into the end of the swimming pool."

Now, I think you'll agree that this man was highly motivated. Once he hit the water, he had a goal to get out and he did. In life, you are going to be thrown out there for the water moccasins and the alligators, but I want to encourage you to keep your eyes on the goal. This system is worth more than any reward you can imagine. It will increase your self-esteem, it will increase your confidence, your knowledge, and your ability to build relationships recalling a person's name.

Stay motivated to practice this system even if you have to imagine alligators chasing you!

My challenge to you is to create more mental journeys like the ones we did with your city and your house. Select different areas of town and memorize 20-30 files on each journey. Perhaps you select five areas of town and 30 files on each journey that will give you 150 files right there!

After this, select five to ten of your family member's homes, friends homes or favorite hang-out spots and build 20-30 files in each of these. Upon completion of these activities you could literally have 300-500 files in a week or so! At the publishing of this book I have around 2900 files!

day 30

Review and a New Beginning

Welcome to the final day! It's Day 30! How are you today? My friend, I have enjoyed this journey. I hope that you have as well. This has been a journey that is not coming to an end; you are now simply taking a fork in the road. This is the beginning of the road, actually. Now is the time that you take what you have learned and you apply it to your life. You are like a bird flying out of the nest. Right now, you should have some motivation to apply this system. If that motivation ever wanes, I encourage you to come back to this course and remind yourself of why you got so excited in the first place. Motivation is an important part of any learning process and I encourage you not to let the learning process end here. And I am not specifically talking about memory training. Although there are some very interesting books and recorded programs on memory training, there is a tremendous amount of knowledge out there at your fingertips.

You could listen to Napoleon Hill's book, <u>Think and Grow Rich</u> or Og Mandino's <u>The Greatest Salesman In The World</u>, or my fellow Texan's book, Zig Ziglar's <u>See You At The Top</u>. And do you know what the exciting thing is? Of the ability to file knowledge shared with you in these trainings to your files and retain the information for as long as you like! That is exciting!

A University of California study reveals that a person living in Los Angeles could acquire the equivalent of a two year college degree in three years of normal driving time by listening to recorded programs. The total amount of time that you invest if you do it while driving would almost be zero! Imagine that! I have never seen a disc jockey jump out of a radio and cut you a check for listening while you are driving, however, every time you listen to a train or an educational program, you get better and better. Now the people who listen to the right recorded programs are the happiest and most well adjusted, excited people I know. Now combine that with a solid reading program and you are really in business. The rule is this. While you are riding, listen and while you are sitting, read.

I recently heard a man I respect very much say that many men desire peace yet few men desire the things that lead to peace. We all want the prize at the end of the tunnel yet few men desire the things that lead to the prize. To get the prize in your life, you must pay the price. The people who listen to the motivational programs, read positive educational books are often the ones who need it the least. They're already successful. When I go to the gym, the people I see there are in such great shape, I wonder why they're in the gym! The ones that are successful in life didn't all of a sudden adopt their reading habits when they were already successful. They are there because of their habits. Good habits are difficult to acquire, but very easy to live with. I encourage you to develop good habits in this educational arena. Constantly challenge your memory with knowledge.

You have a tremendous skill. Very few people have the ability to meet a roomful of people and recall their names, or give a seven hour talk and never access a note, or memorize a chapter of a book, or obtain a list of 65 items after hearing them once. Guys, you have that ability. It is in this system. Whether you know it or not, you have just placed yourself in a very select group. I encourage you to take advantage of this tremendous opportunity. I look forward to meeting you one day and hearing your personal success stories. I enjoyed our journey together and I hope that you did as well.

I will leave you with this thought. It is not what you eat, but what you digest that makes you healthy. It is not what you earn, but what you invest that makes you wealthy. And it is not what you learn but what you remember that makes you wise. My friends, John F. Kennedy paraphrased a verse out of Luke in the New Testament that said, "To those who much is given, much is expected." My friends, you have been given much, now much is expected.

Ron White's Brain Athlete Package:

visit
www.BrainAthlete.com

to learn the details on:

Memory in a Month CD album
Ten minutes a day for 30 days to an unstoppable memory!
◆ ◆ ◆
Speed Reading CD album
Learn to read 1000 words per minute!
◆ ◆ ◆
How to Develop The Mind of Einstein CD album
Discover Einstein's philosophy for success, failure, goal setting,
relationships, time management, humor, success and more
◆ ◆ ◆
Memory Tricks DVD
Instructional video of Ron walking you through the systems that
made him a two time national champion
◆ ◆ ◆
Maximize Your Memory DVD
Two hour memory workshop taught by Ron before an audience.
◆ ◆ ◆
Memory Workshops
attend one of Ron White's public memory workshops

ALSO

Order this book, 'How to Memorize names, numbers, speeches,
playing cards and everything else' in bulk quantity
1-9 $19.95
10-24 $12
25-99 $7
100 plus $3

AUTHORS BIOGRAPHY

Ron White is without question the nation's number one memory expert and one of the tops in the world. He is the two time national memory champion (2009 and 2010) and holds the record for the fastest to memorize a deck of cards in the USA. He has spoken around the world on memory skills in countries such as Puerto Rico, Canada, The Bahamas, Singapore, Malaysia, Bangkok, Spain, Belgium, Australia and even Nebraska.

He has been speaking on memory to business professionals and students since 1991. His talks include, 'Triple Your Memory and Triple Your Business' and 'Memory Power = Student Power'. He has appeared on FOX and Friends, Good Morning America, CBS EARLY Show, ABC World News Tonight, the Martha Stewart Show, CBS Evening News, the Discovery Channel and hundreds of other radio and print media sources.

Ron is also a veteran of the US Navy and served a tour in Afghanistan in 2007.